Raised in East Urban

CHILD CARE CHANGES
in a
WORKING CLASS COMMUNITY

Caroline Zinsser

TEACHERS COLLEGE PRESS

Teachers College, Columbia University
New York and London

Published by Teachers College Press, 1234 Amsterdam Avenue
New York, NY 10027

Funding for this study was provided by grants from the Ford Foundation and the
Hunt Alternatives Fund.

Library of Congress Cataloging-in-Publication Data

Zinsser, Caroline.
   Raised in East Urban : child care changes in a working class
community / Caroline Zinsser.
     p.   cm. — (Early childhood education series)
   Includes bibliographical references and index.
   ISBN 0-8077-3140-4 : $36.95. — ISBN 0-8077-3139-0 (pbk.) : $17.95
   1. Child care—United States—Case studies. 2. Child care
services—United States—Case studies. 3. Working class families—
United States—Case studies. I. Title. II. Series.
HQ778.7.U6Z56 1991
649′.1—dc20   91-23654

ISBN 0-8077-3140-4
ISBN 0-8077-3139-0 (pbk.)

Printed on acid-free paper
Manufactured in the United States of America

98 97 96 95 94 93 92 91   8 7 6 5 4 3 2 1

EARLY CHILDHOOD EDUCATION SERIES
Leslie R. Williams, Editor
Millie Almy, Senior Advisor

ADVISORY BOARD: **Barbara T. Bowman, Harriet K. Cuffaro, Stephanie Feeney, Doris Pronin Fromberg, Celia Genishi, Dominic F. Gullo, Alice Sterling Honig, Elizabeth Jones, Gwen Morgan, David Weikert**

(Continued)

Contents

Acknowledgments

Many people have contributed to this study. I owe most of all to those who must remain anonymous, the parents, caregivers, and others in East Urban who generously and thoughtfully supplied—by answering my questions and telling their stories—the data of this report.

Shelby Miller, of the Ford Foundation, supported this project from its inception, made many helpful suggestions at every phase of the research, and contributed expertise on family day care policy; and Alice Radosh, of the Hunt Alternatives Fund, and Dee Topol, of the American Express Foundation, provided encouragement in a time of need.

Gwen Morgan was enormously helpful in discussions and in her comments on the policy implications of the study. Naomi Fatt, Toni Porter, Ronald Soloway, and Louise Stoney reviewed an earlier version of the manuscript and offered helpful comments and suggestions. Many colleagues in the child care field supplied information about child care arrangements and about debates on regulation. Affiliate members of the New York State Child Care Coordinating Council were especially helpful in this regard.

Susan Blank, Marge Dill, Ellen Galinsky, Judy Gallo, Robert Granger, Sandra Lamm, Maryann Marrapodi, Elisabeth Marx, Fred Merservey, Anne Mitchell, Kathy Modigliani, Toni Porter, and Cynthia Rowe offered comments on a preliminary draft of the Mary O'Malley chapter. Sheryl Dicker, Nancy Kolben, Joan Lombardi, and Tony Ward helped me to sort out the policy issues (although they may not agree with my final recommendations).

Patricia Sutherland, as project assistant, helped with the interviewing and added to the preliminary analysis of the data, and Betsy Andrews transcribed the recordings.

Finally, I would like to thank my friends and colleagues at the Center for Public Advocacy Research, who, during the time we worked together, offered support, advice, insights, and friendship— Leslie Ancrum, Betsy Andrews, Naomi Fatt, Tracy Huling, Betsey McGee, Geraldine Pompey, Rhoda Schulzinger, Ronald Soloway, Lisa Syron, Elaine Tassey, and Constancia Warren.

Raised in East Urban

CHILD CARE CHANGES
in a
WORKING CLASS COMMUNITY

Introduction

Who will care for children while their parents are at work? This question has become the subject of national debate as legislators at federal, state, and local levels wrestle with child care legislation. With child care increasingly accepted as a necessary underpinning of our national economy, what we once viewed as largely the responsibility of families is now studied as a field in need of public policy.

Considering the size of the problem, we have far too little research to help us solve these policy debates. Most child care studies have been conducted in day care centers of preschools, yet this type of care accounts for only about one-fourth of child care arrangements. Almost half is by parents and relatives, including a fourth by mothers and fathers who may take their children to work with them or work in shifts to spell each other in child care. Another fourth is by nonrelatives who are usually family day care providers working in their own homes. According to the most recent Census Bureau data (U.S. Bureau of the Census, 1990), employed mothers whose youngest child was under five used the following as their principal child care arrangement:

> 24%, child's mother of father,
> 22%, child's grandparent or other relative,
> 29%, nonrelatives (22% in a home other than the child's), and
> 24%, day care centers or nursery schools.

These figures show that the most prevalent arrangements for child care are those about which we know the least—arrangements operating outside the sphere of government regulation. Most of this care is by family and relatives who are not subject to regulation. Another segment is by "in-home" child care workers, sometimes called "nannies," who are employed by parents in their own homes and are therefore also exempt from child care regulation. The rest is by family day care providers, commonly known as "babysitters," who care for children in their own homes. Family day care can be by friends and neighbors or it can be by strangers—providers whom parents do not know personally or who are not tied to the community. It is in regard to the latter type of family day care—care by outsiders—that concern for public regulation has been strongest. Almost every state has regulations applying to at least some types of family day care homes, yet most "babysitters" continue to operate outside the regulatory system—because they either are exempt from regulations or choose not to become regulated.[1]

Nonregulated care is sometimes referred to as the "invisible" child care system or the "underground," as though these arrangements were only a shadowy counterpart of "real" child care in licensed settings. Since the public's attention has been directed almost exclusively toward day care centers, many people have come to equate child care only with care in centers, forgetting that the vast majority of child care arrangements are elsewhere. Yet the informality and nonregulated status of this huge segment of the child care market make it particularly difficult as a subject for research. Gaining access to nonregulated child care providers and to the parents who use them is difficult, particularly for the researcher who seeks to interview at length. These arrangements, whether with relatives or with "babysitters," are not likely to be recorded on official listings of providers and are often deliberately kept "off the books" to avoid paying taxes.

If we rely solely on large-scale surveys and quantitative research that can provide us with percentages of use, we may lose sight of the real families in real situations behind the aggregated figures. We will have overall figures for the child care arrangements parents make, but we won't know how people in different communities go about making these decisions, what choices are available to them, and what their standards are for judging the quality of child care. Since licensed care that is also affordable is almost always in short supply, we cannot tell whether parents are deciding on nonregulated care by choice or out of necessity.

What we can't measure through statistics is the cultural framework in which parents and caregivers make child care arrangements—a context that includes their deep-seated beliefs about the role of the family, the place of insiders and outsiders, and how best to bring up children. Statistics indicate racial differences but they say nothing about racial and ethnic identity and the sources of that identity. Surveys can give us a current picture but not the history behind the present situation. It is a premise of this study that standards for and methods of child rearing vary with time (Aries, 1962; Laslett & Wall 1972; Pollock, 1983), with culture (LeVine & White, 1986, Mead & Wolfenstein, 1955; Whiting & Whiting, 1975), and with economic class (Bernstein, 1972; Kohn, 1969; Miller, 1989). Our present convictions about "high quality child care" based on "developmental principles" are also part of an evolving history of child nurture in America (Wishy, 1968) and originate from the white middle class (Ochs & Schieffelin, 1982).

In fashioning child care policy, we cannot make blanket assumptions about how parents make child care choices, nor can we assume that all families will seek a single model of desirable care. We lack information on what different kinds of families in different circumstances would choose for themselves in terms of their own expectations. Although child care is based on the economics of supply and demand, it is by its nature also idiosyncratic in ways affected by life circumstances and culturally determined beliefs. Far from being a monolithic system, child care arrangements result from the complicated and highly variable interaction of small units of demand with small units of supply.

Policy makers must decide what the government's role should be in regard to all forms of child care. To what extent should these differing arrangements be subsidized with government funds? Are these arrangements sufficient to meet most parents' needs? Are these arrangements what parents want? Are parents' expectations changing? Should the government extend and upgrade its regulations? Should regulation be mandatory or voluntary? Until we know more about nonregulated care as well as regulated care—about the parents who use it and the providers who offer it—we will not be able to make wise policy decisions in answer to these questions.

Beyond these questions, which require immediate answers, are more far-reaching concerns. How do child care choices reflect large social and economic changes in American life? In what ways do employment patterns, real estate values, and production shifts within a post-industrial economy affect the balance of child care arrangements? Because deciding how children are to be cared for is a fundamental and central question for any society, any transformation in child care arrangements will not occur overnight, nor will it happen evenly across all segments of the population. No such basic alterations can take place without tension between the old and the new. Child care, considered from this larger perspective, is not only a question of how much and what kind but also a subject for study in its own right, as part of the great changes that have occurred in America over the last century.

This study was designed to examine child care arrangements in one community, with the hope that using a relatively small, circumscribed social setting as a case study, would permit as many of these questions as possible to be addressed. It is a study that is told through stories. The people I interviewed are not meant to statistically represent any one segment of our national population. Although they are undoubtedly similar to many other people living in comparable communities, they speak not as prototypes but as individuals. By recording their stories I hope to document the realities of child care in one community as an illustration of the complexities of forging national child care policies and as an example of how child care is embedded in larger issues of national significance.

METHODOLOGY

The method used in this study is an ethnographic one. Since the study was intended to be of people embedded in and bounded by a system of social relationships within one community, the ethnographic method was particularly suitable. Because the goal of ethnography is to describe a setting in terms of its own internal rules and its meaning for those who are its participants, the data are collected in the field and then analyzed for patterns of behavior that in turn reflect a community's internal values. Werner and Schoepfle (1987), writing about the nature of ethnographic information, state:

> The ethnographer tries to obtain the cultural knowledge of the natives. This knowledge is rarely, if ever, made fully explicit. The nonexplicit aspects of cultural knowledge can often be inferred from casual remarks that must then be clarified by more systematic questioning. The natives, by definition, do not engage in systematic acquisition of knowledge. . . . However, the ethnographer must transcend the accidental and replace it with controlled and systematic data illuminating the intracultural uniformity and variation of cultural knowledge. (p. 23)

Given this objective, the validity of ethnographic research depends on the accuracy with which the data from a specific field situation are collected, analyzed, and described. The value of the research is as a case study and as an example of general theoretical principles rather than as an attempt to delineate a miniature universe that would portray all possible variations of a situation.[2]

Because choosing a suitable site is a crucial element of this type of study, I spent several months investigating possibilities. I did not want to finally select a site until I was confident that I could somehow gain access to cooperative informants. I was also searching for a community characterized by social coherence but not one so insular or specialized as to be completely atypical. I investigated the possibilities of five communities, and in three of these I organized discussion groups with working mothers, not only to give me an idea of the suitability of the community for my study but also to gain more general background information on parents' attitudes toward their child care arrangements (Zinsser, 1987).

I finally selected a community (which I call "East Urban" to protect the identity of my informants) as my study site. Unlike newer communities, where neighbors may not know one another, East Urban had long-established neighborhoods, where the process of change over a period of time could be documented. It was located in a state unusual because it had no regulation of family day care except a newly instituted voluntary registration system. East Urban's only licensed child care was in five day care centers, three of them publicly subsidized, and it was through these, and with the cooperation of a neighborhood health facility, that I was able to establish initial access to the community.

I decided to look particularly at one group within East Urban and chose the white, working- and lower-middle-class families who were first-, second- or third-generation descendants of mainly Italian immigrants and who, I learned, referred to themselves as the "Born and Raised." These Italian-American families formed the predominant ethnic group in East Urban and used relatives, friends, and neighbors for child care. I might have chosen to start with the Latino population, another large group in East Urban and one that also used nonregulated child care, but I was not fluent in Spanish. I deliberately sought working- and lower-middle-class families rather than the very rich or the very poor. Affluent East Urbanites either hired nannies or put their children in private preschools, and the most impoverished East Urbanites (single mothers) were likely to be on welfare and at home. It was the people in the middle I sought—those who were neither so poor as to be eligible for public assistance nor so well off that financing child care was not a major problem.

Because of the nature of the study, I did not use formal delineations (such as educational levels reached or earnings) to define social and economic classes. I termed Born and Raised families, in general, "working class," not only because few attended college and most held blue-collar or low-paying, white-collar jobs, but also because of distinctions concerning where and how people live, which are often described more discerningly by novelists than by social scientists— their neighborhoods, their furnishings, their appearance, their ways of talking, and how they go about organizing their family lives. I did not confine my research to this one group, however. I realized that I would learn more about how child care is arranged within a community by talking to a variety of people representing different racial, ethnic, and economic class divisions and that nonregulated care can be understood only by looking at licensed day care centers as well.

During 7 months of fieldwork I completed 50 formal interviews with community representatives, parents, and caregivers. Whenever possible, I interviewed people where they lived or worked. I reassured them that I would not reveal their identity or even the name of their city in my published study. Each interview was designed to last about an hour, but most lasted longer and a few were shorter. I did not work from a formal list of questions but rather started by eliciting stories. I began by asking parents about their children and asking caregivers about their work. As these accounts unfolded I prompted informants to fill in details of work history and family history so that I had a full picture of each person's employment over the years and how this was balanced with family life.

Twenty-five informants agreed to be audiotape recorded, and I took notes during the other interviews. The formally scheduled interviews were supplemented by many informal conversations with commuters, shopkeepers, bus drivers, people I met in parks, and any other East Urbanites I encountered who were willing to discuss family life. I then transcribed the tape recorded interviews and entered a summary of each, along with my notes on the unrecorded interviews (both formal and informal), my field observations, and my reflections on emerging patterns, into a computerized text-based data management system. Each section of data was indexed according to categories of content and the characteristics of the informant. By this process I was able to derive the categories from the data rather than having to fit my data into preconceived divisions that might not have proved applicable. In presenting the stories that follow, I begin as much as possible, with an objective narrative, using the informants' own words as much as possible, and reserve my interpretive comments until the end of each story or group of stories.

I found informants by word of mouth. Community representatives led me to parents. Parents led me to caregivers, and caregivers to other caregivers. My purpose was to study people who were interrelated by social interactions rather than to study a random sample. By relying on one informant to lead me to another I was able to trace the connections that brought parents and caregivers together and to explore the underlying social structures, as well as individual differences, that determined these choices.

DESCRIPTION OF EAST URBAN

East Urban is a small inland city in the Northeast with the same problems that now characterize many small cities within larger metropolitan areas. Most of the manufacturing firms that once dominated the city's economy have either closed or moved to more favorable locations, eliminating jobs. Affordable housing has become increasingly scarce under the pressures of gentrification. Children of immigrant parents have departed for the suburbs and left an aging population behind. As a result, East Urban's distinctive neighborhoods of working-class, ethnic families, related as kin and sharing common immigrant experiences, are being broken up by a combination of economic and social forces familiar to small, older cities throughout America.

I had always heard of East Urban as a down-and-out place, one of those gray, gritty cities where nobody wanted to live unless they had to, so I was surprised on arrival to find how pleasant and like a small town it seemed. As I stood bewildered on the train platform, unsure of which way to turn, a construction worker came to my rescue, asking, "May I help you? You look puzzled." On Main Street in mid-morning, women shopping for groceries and pushing strollers stopped to chat in the sunshine with an easy familiarity that comes with daily meetings. They not only knew each other but they knew each others' relatives. "Say hi to your mother for me" was a common farewell. The bus drivers seemed to recognize most of their passengers, and I observed one who saved the new hairdo of a woman who had been caught in the rain by reaching behind his seat and pulling out an umbrella, which he earnestly urged her to borrow.

I was used to a city of cement and skyscrapers, but here was a city of low buildings and tree-lined streets. More than 85% of the buildings, I learned, are six stories or less. More than 70% of the housing is more than 50 years old, and much of this dates from East Urban's era of greatest growth at the turn of the century. Some housing, built for prosperous families, consists of attractive brownstones with handsome front stoops leading up to what were originally the parlor floors. But many other buildings were built as tenements with cold water railroad flats to house an immigrant population of unskilled laborers in East Urban's once-thriving factories.

At the corners of many blocks are small low buildings that might be tiny grocery stores, bakeries, or Hispanic or Italian men's social clubs. On other corners, a front door may lead into a long, dark bar, lined with photographs, where men stand and drink. In the rear is a dining room, which can also be entered directly through a side door for women and children, and where older people can remember standing and waiting as children for a pail to be filled with beer for their father at home.

East Urban abounds in signs of ethnic diversity. Its food shops include 14 Hispanic bodegas, nine Italian bakeries, four Asian fruit and vegetable stores, and three Indian grocery stores. The city has 16 Protestant churches—five of them Spanish-speaking congregations and one with a Korean-speaking congregation—five large Catholic churches, and one synagogue. The Catholic churches, where congregations were once all Irish and Italian, now offer services in Spanish as well as English. Annual celebrations also reflect a mixed heritage. The city sponsors parades for St. Patrick's Day, Memorial Day, and Halloween, but there are also three different street processions held in honor of Catholic saints and a fair celebrating Latino heritage.

In many ways, however, the predominant ethnicity of East Urban is Italian. A specialty food shop's sign announces that mozzarella cheese is freshly made three times a day. A bakery window displays announcements of a saint's feast and a pilgrimage to a shrine in Italy. Italian-speaking women in wool coats and kerchiefs crowd the Italian-owned fish store in late afternoon, picking from baskets of crabs, conch, clams, octopus, and squid for the evening meal. A video rental store offers movies in Italian. After a Catholic church's weekly novena, bent old Italian women, dressed in the perpetual black of mourning, linger to talk before hobbling home.

Although East Urban was laid out in a regular grid of intersecting streets, these are not always marked with street signs. It is evidently assumed that either you are in East Urban because you know where you want to go or you shouldn't be there at all. Although the city is small and self-contained, each few blocks constitute their own neighborhood. People refer to "way over on Main Street" when they are only a few blocks away. Neighborhoods are defined by intimate daily contact. To go all the way across town is to make a long journey into unknown territory.

The town occupies about two square miles, with three sides clearly defined. Railroad tracks run along the north. A river runs along the southern border. The "nicer" parts of town are toward the river; the least desirable are backed up against the tracks to the north. To the southeast are East Urban's most handsome homes, the four-story townhouses built for single families, often German immigrants grown prosperous. In the southwest, where once riverside bars and seedy hotels catered to stevedores, urban renewal efforts have resulted in high-rise, middle-class housing and parking lots.

The northeast corner of East Urban is the "worst" part of town. Here city-built subsidized "projects" house the majority of East Urban's small African-American population. Behind, marking the edge of town, run the railroad tracks, where children steal from passing freight cars. In the surrounding streets are the rundown tenements of East Urban's Hispanic population, interspersed with small factories, mainly for the manufacture of clothing. The few remaining large factories are located along the eastern border of town and draw workers from surrounding areas as well as from East Urban. A commuters' train runs regularly between East Urban and the nearby metropolitan city (which I will call the "City").

East Urban has a history, like many similar cities, of successive waves of migration, which have shaped its residential patterns and its economic growth. Rapid population growth began in the beginning of the nineteenth century with Germans who, because they arrived skilled in trades, soon came to dominate the city as merchants, hotel owners, and tavern keepers, as well as workers in the city's building trades and shipping industry. They settled in the more upland, southern parts of town, leaving the swampy lowlands in the north to low-income working classes, many of whom were Irish, the second largest immigrant group. Beginning in the early years of the twentieth century, Italian immigrants poured into East Urban, becoming the dominant ethnic group and giving an Italian-American identity to the city, which it still has.

During the nineteenth century East Urban grew and prospered with a thriving shipping business, a major railroad, and growing numbers of manufacturers. It reached its height of growth and prosperity in the period from 1880 to 1920, with the number of manufacturing firms nearing 400 and the population peaking at 70,000. East Urban manufacturers turned out pencils, varnish, clothing, and other products that could be produced in small brick factories within the confines of a city block. Near the factories, developers built brick tenements for the workers, where they were crowded together, many people to a room, without plumbing or ventilation.

By 1920 East Urban had little land available for new industry and its old brick factories were becoming obsolete. The city's advantages as a rail center vanished with the rise of trucking. Although World War II brought a resurgence of prosperity, the end of the war marked the start of a steady decline in prosperity and loss of population. By 1950 the old brick tenements had become hopelessly dilapidated, driving families who could afford it to seek better housing. During the 1960s and 1970s East Urban lost as many as 1,000 jobs a year. Unemployment finally climbed to the point where about one-quarter of the residents were receiving public assistance.

During these years of shrinking resources, a new wave of immigrants arrived from Puerto Rico, eventually becoming a substantial part of the population and working in unskilled and seasonal jobs in the garment industries that had moved into East Urban's vacant factories and lofts. Since jobs were scarce, these newcomers had an unemployment rate twice as high as the rest of the city and were forced into the worst housing. During this period East Urban had the highest per capita welfare rate, the lowest educational achievement rate, and the lowest incomes in the state.

According to the 1980 census figures, East Urban's total population was about 50,000. The largest number of people identifying themselves as part of an ancestry group were Italian, followed by Irish and German. Eighty percent of the population defined itself as white and 5% as black, but 40% claimed to be of "Spanish origin," including both whites and blacks. The median household income was $11,639, and the median family income $13,650. Twenty-three percent of East Urban's population was earning below poverty level.

In the 1980s a limited part of East Urban's population began to recover. Young professional families who worked in the nearby City started to move into East Urban in a process of gentrification. Attracted initially by low rents and relatively inexpensive row houses on the tree-lined streets, young, affluent career families refurbished crumbling turn-of-the-century buildings or moved into newly converted condominiums. As a result, rents climbed dramatically, and the prices of houses rose so high that many long-time owners sold out and moved elsewhere.

Real estate agencies, clustered around the commuter train terminal post hand-lettered signs in their storefront windows advertising two-bedroom apartments for $700 to $950 a month (the latter billed as "great for shares"). A newly converted condominium is described as being in "historic" East Urban and appealing to the "discriminating sophisticate." These changes are viewed with amazement by long-term residents who remember their town's reputation during the 1950s and 1960s as a "dump" known for its rundown docks and rough street life. One woman born in East Urban commented ironically, "We never knew when we were growing up in a cold water railroad apartment that we were living in a future condominium!"

During the height of the real estate boom, the town buzzed with hints of deals, and even people living in the projects heard rumors that their apartments might be turned into condominiums—as had almost every other available large building, including a former school and church. Gentrification has not been confined to any one part of town but is scattered throughout, wherever real estate developers could persuade owners to sell out. Newcomers appeared to be oblivious to East Urban's social demarcations and would rent or buy any apartment that was available, regardless of its location.

A recent survey of new purchasers of homes shows them to be markedly different from East Urban's former inhabitants. Half are between 26 and 30 years old and more than three-quarters are married with children. Eighty-five percent work in professional, arts, publishing, financial, and sales jobs. Sixty-five percent earn more than $50,000 a year. Estimates of the 1990 census figures show a decrease of perhaps 10,000 people over the past 10 years and a marked increase in median incomes to $18,279 per household. For those who work in East Urban rather than in the City, however, most jobs are still in small manufacturing firms, the unemployment rate is 11%, and decent, affordable housing is difficult to find.

The history of East Urban, which reads much like a textbook account of industrialization in American cities, accounts for a good part of how people live in the city today and how they feel about themselves and their neighbors. Each wave of newcomers seeks better places to live, better-paying jobs, and better chances for their children. But East Urban's early prosperity has disappeared and resources are now limited.

East Urban for many years has had a reputation as a losers' town, and life grows ever harder for its poor and working-class families. Families who grew up here and whose parents live here wrestle with the question of whether to pull up their roots and move on. For those who stay, bound to their disreputable city for whatever reasons, a stubborn and rigid pride comes into play and often defends the old ways against the new, no matter how bad the old may appear to newcomers.

Hard economic realities account for the antagonistic bitterness between economic classes and among ethnic and racial groups that lies below the surface friendliness in East Urban. People identify themselves or others by three main categories: "Born and Raised," "Spanish," and "Americans" (or "Yuppies"). Other, smaller groups are identified as "blacks," "Indians" (or "Hindus"), and "Asians" (or "Koreans"). Born and Raised East Urbanites are white and of predominantly Italian, Irish, and German heritage. The men hold blue-collar jobs, and the women work in service or sales jobs, or as clerks or secretaries. The Spanish group is identified by language. Most are Puerto Rican, but some are from other parts of the Caribbean and from Central and South America. Many of the Spanish group were born and grew up in East Urban but do not identify themselves with the Born and Raised Group. Americans are upper-middle-class, native-born whites. Yuppies, who are also Americans, are the young, affluent newcomers, who work in the nearby City. Although they might be of any race, they are almost all white.

These differences show up in the local weekly newspaper in letters to the editor. Until the late 1970s East Urban was a city of largely foreign-born people or the children of foreign-born parents. Sixty percent of East Urbanites spoke a language other than English at home. The family was at the heart of social life. The newcomers, often young and single, represent another kind of life. One newspaper reader wrote, "Yuppies toil at so-called careers and equate their acquisition of wealth and possessions as a paramount accomplishment of their narrow lives. This is in contrast to traditional views that hold family and rearing of loving, caring offspring as a true meaning of life. East Urban has a new face of wealth and prosperity, but it has lost its soul."

Each of East Urban's self-defined groups has its own distinctive cultural patterns—ways of dressing, of talking, of cooking, of having a good time, of family life, and, significantly for the purposes of this study, of caring for its children.

Chapter 1

Mary O'Malley's Story

I have chosen to begin with the story of "Mary O'Malley" (I have changed all names) because it exemplifies how Born and Raised East Urbanites see themselves: as part of their neighborhood, as workers and participants in East Urban's labor force, as parents caring for their own children, and as providers of child care for others. Mary's story also illustrates the strengths and weaknesses of nonregulated child care that I found characteristic of East Urban. Finally, her account raises issues about child care choices, cost, and quality that are pervasive in East Urban. In line with the ethnographic goal of recording how child care is viewed by those within the community, I have used the title "babysitter" for caregivers who work in their own homes or in the children's parents' homes, because this is the term most commonly used in East Urban.

I first heard about Mary when I interviewed a professional working mother who headed a pediatric unit in a City hospital. This woman commuted from East Urban, and although she was a member of the professional middle class, she had gotten to know some Born and Raised families, whom she would not otherwise have met, through her work in local politics. Hearing that I was seeking Born and Raised caregivers, she remembered hearing Mary's daughter describing her mother's babysitting work. It was through the daughter that I was able to contact Mary and to persuade her to be interviewed.

I found Mary's house on a block of small two-story row houses built in 1885 for railroad and factory workers. Gentrification has so far made little progress here, although the block is beginning to be referred to as a "mews" by real estate agents. The number of newcomers to the block—young professionals seeking small "quaint" houses to restore—is bound to increase, especially since, as Mary told me, there are now 13 widows over age 70 still living in the houses where they brought up their families. But for now the block is still, in the words of a former resident, "85% old East Urban," another way of saying Born and Raised.

These houses are smaller than most in East Urban. Front doors open directly onto the sidewalk, with no stoop. Mary's door was protected by a little entryway decorated with Christmas tree lights, although it was March. She is proud of the fact that she lives in a neighborhood where she doesn't have to lock her door, and I found when I arrived that she had left the front door wide open, protected only by an unlocked outer storm door.

Mary's grandmother came from Ireland to this block. ("She lived to be 97 without a gray hair on her head.") Mary grew up in a neighboring house, and she and her husband have brought up seven children of their own in their present house. Her grown children now live nearby; the youngest two are still at home.

The front door of Mary's house opened into a small living room. Beyond was the kitchen, which also served as a dining room. Since there are only the two rooms downstairs, I wondered how the O'Malleys could fit two adults and their seven children—plus some others in child care—into this small space, but it was neat, and I sensed that it was not just picked up for visitors, but always neat. The front room was decorated most conspicuously and out of obvious pride, with matching graduation photographs of the seven children. On an adjoining wall were the wedding photographs of the ones who had married.

Mary is an energetic 51. She's stocky rather than fat and looks strong and capable. Her hair is short and she's kept it the blond of her youth. Even in her sequin-decorated sweatshirt, worn with pants, she appeared more practical than glamorous. She struck me as not the type to dress up for an interview. From her attitude I got the message, "Here I am, take it or leave it." We sat at her ample kitchen table for the interview, and as we began talking Mary capably finished feeding the baby boy she was taking care of and then put him down for a nap.

Mary has been a babysitter for 11 years, always in her own home. She stayed home with her children when they were small, but when her youngest started Catholic school kindergarten, "I really thought I should go to work, with tuitions and all." She took a job with the county but figured that after taxes she was earning only $75 a week for full-time work and so quit after 6 months. At that point a friend who taught school asked Mary to babysit for her child. This suited Mary. "It was very easy. I liked to be home for my children if something happened. And my mother was getting on in age. She'd always helped me out so I liked being home for her. I was only five doors away." Another advantage was the teacher's schedule, which coincided with the O'Malley children's hours, so that the mother could pick up her child just about when Mary's own children came home from school and could also relieve Mary of babysitting responsibilities during school holidays and vacations.

The most children Mary has taken care of at one time is three, and these were all from one family, the Lorings, whose children were in her care for 7 years. She began caring for one Loring infant at 11 weeks and another at 6 weeks. The parents are professionals; the mother is an executive of a major corporation and the father is a lawyer. Mary took care of the children from 8 a.m. (or 6:30 a.m. if the parents were traveling, which was often the case) until at least 7 p.m.

Although Mary's arrangement with the Lorings was that she was responsible only for feeding the children lunch (and breakfast on the 6:30 days), she usually wound up feeding them supper as well. "With a big family I just cooked, and they usually ate supper here. If they were here, they were here." Mary now misses cooking for seven to ten children. "I don't know what to cook for just Jim and me," she complained. "Just two is crummy."

The Loring family has now moved to an affluent suburb, partly to find a better school system. Mary misses them "like family" and was planning to visit them soon. She said that her older children regarded the little Lorings almost like "their kids" and even included a Loring daughter in one of the O'Malley weddings. Mary's older children would help out by babysitting at the Lorings' at night and by taking Mary's place on the rare occasion when she was sick. The Lorings also miss Mary. They went through seven babysitters since moving from East Urban a year earlier.

At the time the Lorings moved, they were paying Mary $275 a week for caring for their three children, one of whom was in school by that time and needed only after-school care. At the beginning, 7 years earlier, Mary had started at $75 a week. "They always gave me raises. I never had to ask for a raise," she reported with satisfaction. "Even now they give me beautiful gifts at Christmas and on birthdays. They got to be very family. I probably would have done it for nothing."

Mary has found her work for the Lorings and other middle-class, two-career parents satisfying. Her experience taking care of the infant of less affluent parents was less successful.

A minister had called me about a family that needed a baby-sitter very desperately. I said if it was only for a few weeks I would do it. But I didn't want the job. I like one baby or a family. So they brought it down. It was an Indian, and she desperately needed her job and all, blah-blah-blah. I said $75 a week.

When Friday came, the husband came and picked up the baby. They were very irresponsible. They would come very late and forget the time. There was always stories. He gave me the money. I just put it in my pocket and didn't count it. When I did count it, it was $50.

The second week when she came, I said, "You gave me $50." She said, "My husband said that's all I can pay you." I said, "That's not so. It's $75." She said, "I'll speak to him." That went on for 2 weeks, and then I refused the baby. They positively did not pay me the money.

To them it was like that was my share and that was it. I said, "If you want me to babysit, you have to pay me." He said to me, "My wife will have to quit her job." I said, "What do you think *this* is? It's a job." I told them they couldn't pay me what I'm worth.

But most people appreciate you. They were the only strange people I had. And they were people I didn't know. It's nicer if you kind of know the people.

Mary uses her babysitting money "for all these different things the kids need. The extra money for school, the prom dresses. When Catherine got married, I had all the money saved for her shower and her wedding dress and all." She paused and then added with pride, "I gave that to Catherine myself."

Mary likes to babysit in her own home. "It's nice in your own home. You get your place together, and you can go," she said, explaining how she can do her own housework and then take the children on their daily trip to the park. She said of her middle-class clientele, "All new mothers want you at *their* house, they want the baby there, and then after a week they don't care—if they get to know you. The last one was funny," she recalled. "She came to examine the house and meet my family, which was really funny to me. At first she was very particular about me using the changing table and all. After a week it positively was forgotten."

Mary won't babysit on weekends because they are reserved so that her own family can all be together. Her husband has always worked at two full-time jobs. As a maintenance worker in the schools and a postal worker, he leaves home at 7 a.m., comes home for supper from 6 to 8 p.m., and then goes back to work until midnight. "That's why our weekends were always together."

After the Lorings moved away, Mary considered taking an outside job, particularly since her mother died around that same time. Her mother's death affected Mary deeply. They had always been very close, and Mary had taken care of her mother in her old age, visiting her daily. With time on her hands, Mary decided to return to the telephone company where she had worked as an operator before her children were born. She applied and was hired immediately, but she stayed for only 2 weeks before quitting because her husband was "furious" at her for taking the job.

Mary's present babysitting job taking care of a 6-month-old pays $6 an hour, a rate she set "after I found out what everyone else was getting paid." Nevertheless she knows that she should be able to earn more.

> I'm amazed that even when my kids take a part-time job, they make so much money. Maybe I could do that. I just don't know. I keep thinking everyone makes $10,000. Catherine is a secretary. She makes money like an executive. She says the more she makes, the less she does. She never types anymore. She's like an office manager for one of those stock places.

Mary conceded that part of her problem is that she "lacks confidence" in holding an outside job after 30 years of being at home. But of babysitting, she says, "I know I can do that." She ruefully explained her hesitancy and ambivalence, saying, "I threaten to really go to work, and then a baby comes up, and that's it."

At one point, Mary had decided to try working in a day care center as a way to increase her income. She worked for 2 months at a publicly subsidized center but found it unsatisfactory.

> They weren't going to hire me because I was too old, but after the interview they hired me. One question was, "What would you do if a child bit another child?" I said, "I would take that child and probably shake it." They said, "But you can't do that." And I said, "But that's what I would have done." Then they gave me this big interview, and they said I had the job.
>
> The one that ran it, I thought was a little ridiculous. A lovely woman, but you could not have a chair in the room. Even when the children napped. I would go grab a rocker outside and sit down. She called me one day, and she said that I couldn't sit down, that I should clean and polish and do all this. I said, "I'm not cleaning. I'm here to mind children." I don't think that you can't sit on a chair and do things with children. That was ridiculous. You stayed 8 hours. You were dead. Even

the young girls were. And if you sat on the table, she would say, "Tables are made for glasses."

They liked me because I would take care of the babies. We had babies in cribs, and I would feed them and change them. I had no problem with the children at all except it was just an awful lot of work for $8,000 a year. I would take them out for a walk, the ones that could walk. That didn't bother me. But you had to have a project every week do to with these kids. What could you do? The sand table? They were little. They'd say, "Don't you have any imagination?" I took them for a walk. I used to take my group out all the time to the park. I had no trouble.

I didn't like the girl who was the teacher. I said to her, "I didn't know you were a teacher." She said, "Well, I'm not a teacher, but the teacher left so I took over." Everybody was the boss. I thought the girl was the teacher. They said she was the teacher, and I found out she was only there longer than me. Then the girl that took her place, she was the teacher. And for the director to be so grand and so proper, why didn't she have qualified teachers?

It was run very nice, I have to say that. But you get children in there that don't belong. We had a boy that had a problem. He belonged in a special school. And they keep them until they can get rid of them. You were like the referee sometimes. If he took a nap, you'd have to practically lay down beside him and hold him down. That's the bad thing about day care. People are thrown in there that shouldn't be in there. But I have to say the meals were nice, the children were kept cleaner by day care than their families. A couple of kids we would give baths to. Positively needed them.

I called in for St. Patrick's Day off. She told me that I couldn't do that, I could go home early. So I said, "Listen, I'm not coming in. I'm telling you I'm not coming in." And we got into a ridiculous thing like, "These people need their job, and you don't need your job." She had a very odd attitude. Young mothers that were just hanging outside smoking while we were minding their kids. It was nonsense. I was glad I tried it, but they were right. I think I was too old for it.

Mary believes that children grow up best in their own parents' care. They are better disciplined and "turn out better." For her, proof in her own family is that all her children graduated from high school, two are now firefighters, and one is a police officer.

Mary herself grew up as one of seven children. Her father was also a firefighter. Although they were poor, Mary says, "I never thought we missed anything." She remembers that her grandmother, who lived right around the corner, helped out by feeding everyone in the family a big meal every lunchtime. Mary's mother, in turn, took care of her grandchildren. She took one grandson in to live with her because his divorced mother, unlike the other daughters of the family, worked outside the home. Mary described how unusual this single working mother was. "She worked until the day she had him and was back to work 3 weeks after, which was a big deal with the whole community. Even her divorce was something that we never mentioned. Never. My father never mentioned that divorce in the house." Mary's mother had 21 grandchildren, and "there was always some child hanging around. There was a crib in her room as long as I can remember. When I got married, in the bridal pictures there's a crib in the background."

Now Mary herself is a grandmother, but times have changed. Two of her sons have children, and their wives plan to work outside the home. One daughter-in-law, Stephanie, "had a very good job" before she married and had a baby. She now goes part-time to nursing school at night while her husband cares for their son. "And if they ever get stuck," Mary assured me, "we're right here." Since two of the O'Malley sons live in the same apartment house right around the corner, the wives also use each other for fill-in babysitting. "Very rarely do they have any problem," said Mary, "but the family's always here."

The other daughter-in-law, Cheryl, left her job as a secretary for a local firm when her first son, Danny, was born. When Danny was three, she returned to work at her old job and left him with Mary, who at that point had just ended her brief stay at the day care center. When Cheryl's second son, Frank, was born, she went back to work sooner, partly because she was able to arrange to work only Tuesdays, Wednesdays, and Thursdays during the summer when Danny is on vacation from school. During the summer months Mary takes Danny to her bungalow at the seashore, and Cheryl joins them for 4-day weekends. To Mary's disappointment, Cheryl has put the younger boy, Frank, with another babysitter.

Mary could only guess why Cheryl and her husband didn't ask her to take care of both children, because she has never confronted them for their reasons, but she thinks she knows the answer. "They couldn't afford to pay me what the others were paying me, I'm sure. I think that's what bothered them. But I wouldn't have taken the money. They never asked me." Cheryl and her husband pay their babysitter $60 a week, which includes food, for full-time care.

Mary described Cheryl's babysitter, Anna, in almost awesome terms. Anna takes care of about 10 children and charges whether they come or not. Since this was the only person in East Urban that I'd heard of who was taking care of so large a group as to be illegal, and since her terms were more rigid than those of anyone else that I had talked to, I was eager to learn more about Anna.

When I said I'd like to talk to Anna, Mary quickly said that would be impossible because Anna would be afraid of penalties for running an illegal operation, but Mary readily offered to call Cheryl at her office so that I could talk to her about Anna. After Mary reached Cheryl and handed me the telephone, I found it awkward to start the interview. Cheryl seemed to me to be a little resentful of being put on the spot in this way by her mother-in-law and repeated what Mary had said about not wanting to give me the babysitter's number or where-abouts. But she agreed to answer some of my questions.

Cheryl said she had known Anna for about 10 years, dating back to the time when they lived in the same building and Anna began her babysitting business with two or three children. By expanding her business, Anna was able to buy a house and to renovate it so that two rooms are used as children's playrooms. When Frank was a toddler and Cheryl decided to return to work, she made an appointment to visit Anna. Cheryl liked what she saw and put Frank's name on the waiting list. She had to wait only 2 months, although the wait is usually a year. Anna takes care of "about 10" children and has free places only when a child "graduates," usually to Catholic school kindergarten. She likes to be able to care for children continuously from infancy until they enter school.

"I love her," said Cheryl. "She's like a grandmother. When you walk in, you smell something she's cooking in the kitchen. She has a nice yard. She loves the children like they were her own grandchildren. It's not like a school." When I asked Cheryl how she would compare this with licensed day care centers, she said that Anna's was better because centers have a "colder atmosphere and more people." In contrast to centers, she sees Anna's care (even with one caregiver for 10 children) as "one-to-one." As an example of the kind of care she likes, Cheryl described how Anna gives each child a birthday party.

I asked Cheryl how she could tell that Anna was a good baby-sitter. "Anybody who knows her says there's no bad thing. It's just like Frank is with family," Cheryl said. "When he leaves, he hugs and kisses Anna." Cheryl added that her son's behavior had improved since he started staying with Anna. "When I first brought my son to her, he was a little brat. Now he's fine. And the only punishment she uses is to stand them in the corner for being fresh. My son loves her." I asked how Anna could manage to care for 10 young children at once, and Cheryl laughed. "My husband swears she drugs them," she said jokingly.

After I had ended the telephone call to Cheryl, I asked Mary if she had ever considered taking a large group of children. "Oh, never," she answered emphatically. "I don't know how Anna does it. She trains the children. She gets them off the bottle and everything. She's amazing. She has two rooms downstairs in the house. They're just playrooms, and the children have to bring their own sleeping bags. But she's one in a million. In the summer she hires someone so they can go out in the yard. They don't go out in the winter at all. They watch TV. They learn things."

Halfway through our interview we were interrupted by the arrival of Mary's grandson, Danny, home from first grade in his Catholic school uniform. Mary usually walks him to her house, but on the day of the interview someone had given him a ride. When I asked Danny about school, Mary interjected, "He got first honors twice now. Did you get your report card this week yet?" she asked, obviously ready to show it to me. Danny said that report cards would be given out on Wednesday and then went into the living room, where he settled down near the sleeping baby to watch television.

About half an hour later we were interrupted by another visitor, a woman Mary's age, who entered without knocking. This was Danny's other grandmother, Cheryl's mother Dorothy, who lives in the same apartment building as her daughter. She has a part-time job but is also a babysitter. Every weekday she picks Danny up from Mary's house after school. From there they go to pick up another child at his school so that Dorothy can care for both children together. Dorothy takes care of the other boy as a paid babysitter. (I did not learn whether she was also paid for her regular after-school care of Danny.)

The two grandmothers, who have known each other for years, chatted for a few minutes in the kitchen. Mary, who had by this time become interested in the child care questions I'd been asking, asked Dorothy how as a young, widowed mother she had managed to hold a job and to care for her son. Dorothy explained that she had worked for a local construction company where she could take her son with her to the office and where there was plenty of play space in an adjoining garage for him to run around in.

Soon after Dorothy and Danny left, the mother whose baby boy Mary was taking care of arrived to pick him up, bringing along her two older children whom she had just picked up from school. When she heard that I had been interviewing Mary about child care, she told me that she is "very fussy" about who babysits for her. She had spotted Mary picking up a child from school and asked around to find out who she was.

By this time Mary's own two children who live at home had arrived and were sprawled in front of the television set, along with the two other schoolchildren. I was surprised to realize we had now accumulated three adults, two children, two teenagers, and a baby in the tiny living room, but everyone appeared to be relaxed and to accept this as routine. Perhaps in this household, eight is minimal.

After the baby's mother had collected all three of her children and left and I had made preparations to leave myself, Mary became reflective. She said, "It's different now with my mother gone. Now I just have so much free time. I'm bored sometimes. When this mother asked me to babysit, I swore I wasn't going to do it. But as soon as I did, I liked it again." She paused, leaned back in her chair, and appeared to think over her alternatives at this point in her life. Then she leaned forward, putting her elbows on the table, and smiled broadly. "You know, I'd like a little granddaughter. *That's* what I'd like."

CHILD CARE

With each generation Mary's family has changed its child care arrangements. Mary's mother cared for her seven children full-time and never took a job outside the home. Mary's grandmother shared the work by feeding the whole family a big mid-day meal every day during the children's noon recess from Catholic school. When Mary's oldest sister, who was employed, went back to work soon after her son was born, the neighborhood was scandalized. Mary's mother raised that grandson, who was not very much younger than her own youngest children. Because the family was large and the children were born over a long time span, an extra child could be integrated into the household without too much disruption. When women routinely cook for 10, adding another child or two to the table is not that much of a problem. Child care was shared work between generations but always within the maternal family.[1]

Mary's own child care followed a different pattern. She stayed at home to care for her children full-time when they were preschool age, but after the youngest had entered school, she began to care for other people's children as well as her own. Her daughters sometimes shared in this work. When Mary's children married and had children of their own, Mary also took care of her grandchildren, but mainly on a part-time basis. Care of children was still shared across generations but was no longer confined to family members only.

The next generation follows still another pattern. Mary's daughters-in-law, who are unable to take care of their children full-time because of job commitments, use a variety of child care arrangements. Now that babysitting has become a form of employment, choices of child care may be determined by how much it costs. This newest generation of mothers still uses family members to care for infants and toddlers but is beginning to rely on outsiders to care for preschool children. Although these generational changes show a movement away from care within the family to care for and by outsiders, the model for child care is still the family. Mary is proud of the fact that her relationship with the Lorings was like family.

The Lorings were Mary's employers but they were also bound by emotional ties. Mary manages this duality of treating a business arrangement as though it were a family relationship by maintaining an ambivalent attitude toward her earnings. Although she says that she would work for the Lorings "for nothing," this may just be a way of saying that she prefers to think of her relationship in terms of nurturing family affection rather than working for income. She prefers the Lorings's paternalistic method of periodically granting raises to a negotiating process between employer and employee, and she values the gifts she receives in addition to her monetary pay.

Mary's daughter-in-law Cheryl also seeks a family relationship with her professional babysitter Anna. Cheryl says that she and her son Danny love Anna "like a grandmother" and that Anna in turn "loves the children like they were her own grandchildren." Even though Anna takes care of "about 10" children, Cheryl sees this as a "one-to-one" relationship. Perhaps because of past generations of large families, Cheryl sees Anna's caring for 10 in her own house and yard, with the smell of cooking wafting from her kitchen, as a continuation of idealized family bonds.

By contrast, Cheryl views professional center-based care as "colder," that is, lacking emotional ties. One of her reasons for liking Anna's program is that "it's not like a school." In describing why she liked Anna's program, Cheryl did not mention early learning or socialization. Instead, she repeatedly emphasized the personal, rather than the professional, values.

Since mother–daughter bonds are especially strong (in contrast to Mary's ties with Cheryl, who is a daughter-in-law), it may be that when

Mary's daughters have children they will leave them with Mary full-time. Mary seems disappointed that Cheryl has chosen a babysitter from outside the family, but what she really wants is to take care of a granddaughter. It seems that Mary, who has recently lost the daily companionship of her mother, would like to fill the loneliness of that gap by caring for yet another relative from the newest generation.[2]

EMPLOYMENT

Child care in Mary's family has been closely linked to employment, and employment patterns, like those of child care, have changed over three generations. Mary's parents were able to bring up seven children on the single income from Mary's father's work as a firefighter. Mary's mother took it for granted that her work would be within the home unless, for some reason, she lost her husband's financial support. Her job was to take responsibility for the care of her husband, her children, her parents, and her grandchildren as well as for the housework.[3]

Although Mary's husband works at two full-time jobs, she felt that once her youngest child was in school, she should add to the income of the household. Mary considers her earnings as necessary to meet the children's expenses, particularly those that might be considered "marginal" but are important to Mary as things she feels her children deserve—parochial schooling, prom clothes, and bridal showers.

Mary has some record of employment outside the home. She worked as a telephone operator before her children were born, and has since held, for short periods, jobs with the county, in a day care center, and with the telephone company. But Mary appears to prefer her babysitting job because it also allows her to fulfill her traditional responsibilities of housework and caring for her mother, husband, children, and grandchildren.

Mary's attitude toward her babysitting job reflects her ambivalence toward employment. Not only does she choose work that will allow her to continue to fulfill her familial duties, but her work entails further nurturance of other people's children. In her relationship with her employers, the Lorings, Mary is proud of the fact that she never talked about money. She likes to think of herself and the children she cares for as "family" so that the payment does not appear to be the main object. To Mary, what she receives for babysitting, from either within the family or without, is like the traditional "egg money" of farm women—cash earned on the side by wives who then have exclusive control over how it is spent. It pleases her to be able to work for families who have the ability to pay what she considers a fair fee. At the same time she realizes that most jobs outside the home pay more than she is able to earn from babysitting.[4] She still thinks of $10,000 a year as a good salary and finds it hard to imagine herself earning the salaries that women, such as her daughter, are now able to earn.

Mary also lacks confidence to take employment other than child care. She knows she's a good babysitter but thinks of herself, at 51, as too old to begin any new kind of work. Her attempt to return to her old job, working for the telephone company, was thwarted by her husband's opposition. Although Mary thinks about other work, it seems likely that she will stay in child care, particularly if she can combine this with taking care of her daughters' children.

Two of Mary's daughters-in-law are mothers. Although, unlike Mary and her mother, these young mothers are planning to work full-time, their job choices reflect dual commitments toward mothering and earning income. Nursing, a nurturing profession, can be studied and practiced on schedules flexible enough to enable husband and wife to share child care. Cheryl's job is local, so that she works close to home and has been able to arrange with her long-time boss for time off in the summer to care for her children during school vacations.

Employment over three generations has changed from a husband supporting a family on a single income, to a husband who holds two full-time jobs and is helped by his wife's part-time work at home, to husbands who count on their wives' full-time, out-of-home employment to support their young families. The women, although they have moved into paid work, have chosen jobs that reflect their traditional values of helping others and of work within the household.

HOUSING

Houses on Mary's block were built to be inexpensive. They are smaller than most in East Urban and lack central heating, but even so, Mary's children's generation cannot afford to buy a house on the block where they grew up. Of course, they may not want to. Though newcomers may find the block houses quaintly old-fashioned, young adults who grew up on the block in large families cramped into small spaces may see these same houses as uncomfortably old-fashioned.

Where the block used to be teeming with children from large Catholic families, there are now few. A former block resident describes how it used to be. "It was small, one-family rowhouses, and everybody knew everybody, and half of them were related to each other. You were never alone. Everybody kind of looked out for every-body's kids." Because there was practically no through traffic, it was relatively safe for children to play in the street under adult supervision. When children's mothers were away, other neighbors, who often were relatives, took responsibility.[5]

Although the younger generation is moving away from their par-ents, in Mary's family they still live nearby. Two of Mary's son's families, along with other relatives, live in the same apartment house around the corner, so that family members are still close at hand for babysitting. But arrangements are no longer informal; they must be set ahead of time.

Child care is further complicated by the architecture of modern apartment houses. Living space is physically removed from children's outdoor play space, and elevators are further barriers. The old block with its unlocked front doors opening directly onto the street was much more amenable to communal child care.

TRADITIONS OF CHILD REARING

In the O'Malley family, as in other East Urban Born and Raised families, what was good enough for your parents should be good enough for you. In contrast to the middle class, Born and Raised families do not always aspire to upward mobility. Mary says with satisfaction, "My father was a fireman, my three brothers are firemen, and now I have two firemen. I guess we're just East Urban people." Her implication is that the O'Malleys are people who "know their place" and are comfortable with it.

In Mary's view, families know best how to bring up their children. She does not talk about early learning before parochial school kinder-garten and did not send her children to preschool. In her babysitting job Mary stresses family rather than educational values. Her ideal is to treat the children in her care as she would her own children, to keep them safe by careful supervision and to keep them healthy by daily trips to the park, cleanliness, and generous feeding.

When Mary took a job in the day care center, she found that her traditions of child care differed from those of her professionally trained director. She thought the "babies" she cared for were too young for the weekly "projects" she was required to devise. To Mary, going for a daily walk was enough, as long as there was "no trouble." Mary also disliked being told to do things in ways that seemed to violate her sense of how they should be done. The professional standards seemed to her "ridiculous," a way of making the work more complicated than it needed to be.

Mary and Cheryl both admire Anna, the babysitter, for her traditional ways with children—punishing them by having them stand in the corner and rewarding them with hugs and kisses. Mary makes the point that Anna "trains" the children. The O'Malleys believe that children should be deferential to adults and not "fresh." More middle-class goals for child rearing, such as creativity and independence, are not mentioned.

When Mary talks about learning, it is in terms of learning from television or bringing home a good report card. The goal of education in this family is to graduate from high school in order to get a decent-paying job.

CLASS AND ETHNICITY

Mary lives on a block built for railroad and factory workers and still characterized as working class. Its residents typically take blue-collar jobs after completing high school, and Mary's husband falls into this pattern. Being "poor," in Mary's view, does not mean a family "missed anything."

Mary's first babysitting job came from a mother who taught school, and her most successful stint of babysitting, with the Lorings, was for high-income professional parents. She has also worked for other professional couples, and her name is now passed from one to another. When Mary says, "It's nicer if you kind of know the people," she is referring to this network of middle-class parents.

By contrast, the Indian family, Mary says, "were the only strange people I had." It seems likely, although she did not say so outright, that Mary was prejudiced against the Indians because of their ethnicity. They also represented an alien culture. Her dealings with the family appear to have been fraught with cross-cultural misunderstandings. Where the Lorings were valued as family and terms of employment were not discussed, the Indian father was told, "What do you think this is? It's a job." Mary's work for middle-class families, whose high earnings enable them to pay regularly and in full, was markedly different from her work for the lower-earning Indian family who expected her to charge only her "share" of the wife's earnings.

When Mary went to work at the day care center, she found she resented being treated as an inferior by the professional director, "so grand and so proper." The director's admonition that "tables are made for glasses" could be viewed as a class-based reproach. When the director told Mary to "clean and polish," Mary may have felt that was beneath her. She resented the class distinctions represented by the professional standards of the center. It only added to her hostility that the classroom teachers lacked the credentials that would at least have provided them with a sanctioned status for assuming authority.

If Mary was unable to identify with the professional staff at the center, she did not identify with the center parents either. Behind Mary's description of "young mothers that were just hanging outside smoking while we were minding their kids" lies her disapproval of unmarried teenage mothers on welfare. The ways of these parents are not Mary's ways. Some of their children do not even meet her standards of cleanliness, to her a primary failing in proper child care.

Mary's unease came to a head when she, acting on traditional Irish solidarity, asked for St. Patrick's day off. The director, in denying her request, seemed to Mary to be putting the parents' jobs ahead of Mary's. When Mary, as a result, quit the center job, saying, "I think I was too old for it," she left a situation of class and ethnic conflict that she identified with new social patterns too difficult for her to accept.

In providing a service to white professional parents, Mary positions herself as below the upper middle class but above the nonwhite working class. When asked to provide her service to those "below" her, as she was when caring for the Indian baby and working in the day care center, she was resentful and ended the arrangements.

CHOICES, COSTS, AND QUALITY

It is clear that the O'Malley family will need some kind of child care. In the new generation of young parents, both mothers and fathers are working outside the home in response to long-term and irreversible changes in community and national economic forces. Yet it seems unikely that this family will use licensed, center-based care for their children.

Their ideal of quality care is what can be provided within the family, but to a large extent they are being forced to turn elsewhere because of work schedules and family finances. In Cheryl's family, one grandmother works part-time and is available for child care only during after-school hours. The other grandmother, Mary, earns fees from parents outside the family that cannot be matched by her own relatives.

Since they must deal with outside caregivers, the family has chosen a well-known neighbor, even though they recognize her child care as an illegal arrangement. Anna's group operation is unlicensed and therefore illegal, but even if Anna had wanted to be licensed for group family day care, there is no such license offered by the state.

Fees for child care in day care centers would, in any case, be a problem. With their combined incomes, the young O'Malley parents would earn too much to be eligible for subsidized care but too little to afford the $336 a month fees charged by private centers for the full-time care of preschoolers. Although they cannot match the fees paid to Mary by the Lorings, they can afford Anna, who is able to keep her fees down by caring for an illegally large group of children. And what the Lorings pay Mary, though it is more than the young O'Malleys can pay, is still less than what they would pay for three children at a licensed private center.

The young O'Malley family's earnings, though nowhere near the Lorings's, are too high to qualify for subsidized care, and yet the O'Malleys do not benefit from the tax policies designed to help working parents. They do not declare their child care expenses for a dependent care tax credit because that would necessitate naming Anna as their caregiver and would expose her to charges of illegal operation. Mary has never asked the Lorings whether they claim a dependent care tax credit or receive child care benefits from their employers, one of which is a large corporation. Considering their very high salaries, however, it is clear that even without these means of offsetting child care expenses the Lorings could well afford Mary's services. They paid a lower proportion of their combined income for child care than Mary's own children, who use lower-cost illegal care, do. This would be true even if child care expenses were measured as a percentage of the mothers' incomes alone, rather than of the combined household earnings. (Most working mothers figure what they can afford to pay for child care on the basis of their own paychecks, not as a percentage of the combined household income.[6])

Mrs. Loring, who holds an executive job with a large corporation, was able to purchase safe, conscientiously provided care, including infant care, for her three children at a relatively low price. She also had care that met her job's requirements of travel and extended hours. When her children were sick, she had someone to care for them so that she did not have to take time off from work. She was able to perform as a corporate executive because of the child care available to her. Yet her corporation did not directly support Mary's work. It was Mary's low fees and flexible hours that indirectly supported the corporation.

Cheryl's employer, on the other hand, is a small businessman with no parental leave policy or formal child care benefits. When Cheryl stayed at home with her children until they reached toddler age, the family had no second income. She was fortunate, however, to be able to return to her old job because she had a favorable work record, which also helped her to work out an arrangement for part-time work to accommodate her child care needs without a reduction in salary. In effect, her employer subsidizes the school vacation time that she spends with her children. (However, without these arrangements Cheryl, a highly valued employee, would not have returned to her job after the birth of her second child.)

Operating completely outside any system of supervision, neither Anna nor Mary is subject to health and safety regulations for the protection of the children they care for, and neither has professional training. The quality of the babysitting that Mary provides, however, satisfies family members and the Lorings, who through their long association with her have become like family. Mary's care may not be professional but it is loving and reliable, and it reinforces family and local community values. To this extent, child care providers like Mary O'Malley form an essential part of East Urban's child care system.

But there are also problems in Mary's story. We learn that Cheryl has turned to illegal care, that the Indian family has been turned away, that only professional career families can afford Mary's services. Child care in East Urban today is no longer provided solely within the family or between friends; questions of negotiating the terms of child care between strangers undermine what was once a self-sufficient system. Mary's story raises issues of social and economic change that I found borne out again and again in my interviews with East Urbanites.

Chapter 2

Born and Raised Parents
Talk About Child Care

When I had identified the various groups in East Urban, I found that members of my target group for study, the Born and Raised, were clustered in distinctive neighborhoods. They were mainly descendants of Italian, and some Irish, immigrants who lived in the same neighborhoods where they were born. My problem soon became how to find members of the Born and Raised group who would agree to be interviewed about child care. I found that there is little social interaction between racial and ethnic groups in East Urban and that Born and Raised families stick to themselves. They act as a society within a society. Most of their social relations are with other members of their families. They also have a mistrust of outsiders prying into their affairs. What they do, they consider their own business and no one else's. Community and family provide guides to behavior, not advice from outside authorities, and they had no incentive to cooperate in an academic study, no matter what its purpose.[1]

Another problem with gaining access to Born and Raised informants was that the terms in which I was defining my study were not those that Born and Raised families would ordinarily use in describing themselves. They do not see themselves as parents who depend on "day care." In fact, they do not even use this term as it is commonly used by professionals to apply to a wide variety of programs, including family day care. In Born and Raised terms, child care falls into two categories—care by "babysitters" or in "the day cares," which is what they call day care centers. Nor do Born and Raised mothers readily identify themselves as "working mothers," because the idea of women in paid work is at variance with the idealized family in which the mother stays at home, at least while the children are young, and the husband's earnings support the family. Working wives were ambivalent about their employment, and discussions on the subject were not easy for them. Often, after I had explained the nature of my project, Born and Raised women would say they knew of no one who would "fit." Their attitude was, if it's a study about working mothers and day care, then it's not about us.

Eventually I was able to find 14 Born and Raised parents who agreed to be interviewed about child care. Some of these I met in the outer offices of city administrators. These women, usually married to blue-collar workers, held jobs as secretaries, clerks, and receptionists and were somewhat experienced in dealing with the general public. I increasingly realized that the "true" Born and Raised families—those who were most conservative in preserving past values—were inaccessible to my prying eyes. In the main, parents I talked to tended to be the ones who were most open to outsiders, either through the nature of their work or because they had adopted an independent stance against traditional family patterns. They were the ones who were adapting to changes in the traditional patterns of family life and were willing to discuss what those changes entailed.

TOMMY: "YUPPIFIED ITALIAN"

Tommy was not yet a parent, but he was engaged to be married and had definite opinions about his "very heavy Italian" family life. And more than most Born and Raised that I interviewed, he was able to articulate his viewpoint and to say where he stood in relation to the rest of the world. I learned about Tommy when I went to the weekly East Urban newspaper offices to ask local reporters if they knew any Born and Raised parents. They suggested Tommy, who worked in the newspaper's advertising office, as the archetypical Born and Raised spokesperson. The reporters assured me that Tommy not only would be willing to be interviewed but would actually enjoy talking about his Italian heritage. This proved to be the case.

As an East Urbanite who has risen from a blue-collar background to a white-collar job (although he continues to work nights as a cook in a delicatessen), Tommy moves between his Born and Raised family and friends and his new professional colleagues. He has capitalized on his dual status by writing occasional feature articles for the newspaper, what he calls "fluffy articles," in which he reports as an expert on "native" East Urban customs, such as local nicknames and Italian cooking.

In his position as a bridge between two East Urban social and economic groups, Tommy is reflective and articulate about the differences between his two worlds. He began our interview, for example, by explaining, "I was born and raised in downtown East Urban where we 'berl' water, use 'tinferl,' and go to the 'terlet.'" This had the ring of an old joke, and I had the impression that although Tommy's observations were acute, they were perhaps exaggerated in the service of his self-proclaimed role as a "colorful" Born and Raised spokesperson. He indicated repeatedly that he is not afraid to say what he thinks, regardless of what others might consider indiscreet.

Tommy is a third-generation East Urban Italian. His father was a teamster whose job was loading trucks and his mother was a housewife who stayed at home to care for Tommy and his brother. Tommy, however, has planned a different family life. His fiancee is planning to combine motherhood with a job, even though, as Tommy was quick to assure me, they could "live nice" on his earnings alone. They plan to use the older generation of maternal relatives for child care—either the children's maternal grandmother or a maternal aunt who is already watching a grandchild of her own. Tommy explained why.

> It's just that we do everything within the family unit. We're heavily family-oriented. Our whole life is around the family. In America, people don't really have that. It's nothing for an American child to grow up and move to California while their family is in East Urban. For us, it's a travesty. You have to be near your family. Holidays, everything is around the family. There's no such thing as going out with your wife on New Year's for dinner alone. It has to be with ten thousand people.

Tommy was eager to tell me why family life was central to his group and how traditions of child rearing were important for the continuity of a value system. He can count on relatives for this, he explained, but not on strangers.

> My particular group that I come from are very conservative, yuppified Italians, if you want to look at it that way, who still believe in the family. If it was good enough for Grandma and good for Mama, it's good enough for me. I believe that if the child grows up like me and my mother and my mother's mother and my father's father, they're going to be good no matter what. I grew up okay, they'll grow up okay. The child has the same potential I had under the same system.
>
> I would rather spend the same amount of money with relatives than with the day care system. I can trust them. I can

sleep easier knowing the child is with a relative than with strangers. Discipline is: you get hit if you do something wrong—if you do something good, you get praised. It's the basic, old-fashioned, what's right is right, what's wrong is wrong. Walk the straight and narrow.

Tommy estimated that he was related to about 100 people in East Urban, and he said that none of them use day care centers. He had not realized that it was possible for children younger than three to be enrolled in centers. When I explained that even infants can be cared for in center-based programs, he reacted dramatically, "Get out! Really? That's retarded! That's disgusting! I think that's horrible! Why have a baby?" When I pointed out that some working parents require center-based infant care, Tommy conceded that he would not "look down on a welfare mother who had to support her kids" if *she* put her baby in an infant program. "People have to do what they have to do," he said, but it was clear that Tommy does not plan to be one of them.

*   *   *

Even though Tommy recognizes himself as in transition from his working-class parents to a white-collar job, a "yuppified Italian," he takes pride in his ethnic heritage and makes a point of separating himself from the "American" way. He would not, for example, want to move away from the neighborhood of his birth. It is in the home community that Italian culture is transmitted.

Child rearing is the vehicle for passing this culture from one generation to the next. The system that produced the previous generation should be good enough for the next. Standards of right and wrong are reinforced by reward and punishment. Tommy wants his future children to "walk the straight and narrow," for to depart from these time-worn paths of authoritative discipline would be to risk failure.

Tommy sees the "old-fashioned" value system as what has enabled East Urban's immigrants to gain economic security. But their status is not so firm that they can ignore a real possibility of falling into poverty. Day care centers, in Tommy's view, are for children whose parents have failed—failed in their family relationships, like "American" parents, or failed within the economic system, like "welfare" parents.

Tommy's acceptance of his fiancee's decision to take a job is a departure from his family's tradition, but his attitude toward child care is firmly rooted in the past. Tommy is comfortable with the idea that his wife will work only because he knows that his children can be cared for by their maternal relatives. With his large family living nearby there is no need to seek care from strangers, either babysitters or in the day cares.

SUZANNE: "IDEAL" CHILD CARE

Tommy had definite opinions about child care, but he was not yet a parent. Suzanne, a Born and Raised working mother, has had 9 years of combining employment with child care. She is a secretary-receptionist in a small office dealing with urban renewal, where I had gone seeking census tables. When she offered to help me photocopy some charts I needed, I took the opportunity to ask her about child care in her own family.

Suzanne agreed to be tape recorded, probably because she saw the project as something that interested her boss. The interview was difficult because Suzanne offered no information beyond what I elicited. She was guarded and circumspect in her answers and appeared to be protecting her family. She presented a problem-free picture of child care arrangements that were made without stress and to everybody's satisfaction.

Suzanne and her husband have two children, a boy of 12 and a girl of nine. Before the children were born, Suzanne worked full-time, but after the birth of her son she stayed at home until he was three before returning to work part-time. With the birth of her second child she stayed at home only 9 months before returning to part-time work. Child care was provided by her mother, who lived nearby and took care of the children in her home, where Suzanne dropped them off by car every day. If they were sick, the grandmother would come to Suzanne's house to care for the children. Since both sets of grandparents lived in Suzanne's neighborhood, she always had backup arrangements.

Suzanne said of her child care, "It's ideal, you know. You can trust family." She said that although the grandmother was a "little bit more liberal" in child rearing than Suzanne might have wanted, there were no major disagreements because grandmother care "isn't that big of an impact." When I asked if the grandmothers were paid, Suzanne said no, and explained, "We're a close family. We help each other." In her neighborhood, Suzanne said, all young children go to their grandmothers' homes for babysitting.

As her children approached school age Suzanne began to worry that they needed a "school-type atmosphere" and to "get used to working with groups." She put the children in Head Start and served on its board, but was concerned that "they should have been doing less play and more prep toward education." When the children reached kindergarten age, Suzanne sent them to St. Margaret's, the Catholic school of her family parish. Although Suzanne doesn't consider herself "particularly religious," she wants her children to receive the sacraments and have some exposure to religious education. She and her husband also consider parochial schools better than public schools at getting students into college.

Suzanne now works full-time. Since the grandmother lives only two blocks from the parish school, she can pick up the children and provide after-school care. Suzanne's husband recently decided that their son was old enough for his own latchkey. He has begun to feel too "restricted" with his grandmother and wants to be with his own toys and computer games after school. The younger sister still stays with her grandmother. During the summer months both children are at home by themselves. They have only one neighbor who lives nearby and would be available during the day to help them in an emergency, because the others work. Of course Suzanne could easily arrange to come home quickly from her East Urban office if the children summoned her.

*   *   *

For Born and Raised working mothers the maternal grandmother is often the most acceptable child care provider except for parents. Since child care is primarily the mother's responsibility, she counts on her mother to provide the same child rearing that she herself received. The Born and Raised working mothers I interviewed want their children's upbringing to be identical to their own (unlike many of their middle-class counterparts, who told me how they disapprove, in retrospect, of their parents' ways). Suzanne reported only one area of disagreement—her mother was a "little bit more liberal," which can probably be attributed to affectionate indulgence. In general, they agreed on family-accepted norms for children's behavior so that grandmother care did not appear to Suzanne to make "that big of an impact." Suzanne stayed at home with her oldest child for 3 years, but when her second child was born she felt confident enough about her child care to return to work after only 9 months.

The grandmother's child care was lacking in one important respect, however. When Suzanne's oldest child reached preschool age she decided he needed a group experience as preparation for school. Suzanne used Head Start as a preschool, even serving on its board. She and her husband are ambitious for their children's educational success, pay their Catholic school tuition, and expect them to go to college. For the important task of school preparation, grandmother's care was not enough.

Another potential problem is Suzanne's reliance on latchkey care. Suzanne's son is no longer content to stay with his grandmother and now goes home by himself. The children are also left alone during the summer, when the grandmother is away. Although the family lives in a "nice" part of town, neighbors who were once available as adults who could "keep an eye" on Suzanne's children are now at work themselves. Even Suzanne's "ideal" child care has its limitations.

MARJORY: TWO GENERATIONS OF WORKING MOTHERS

One of the first places I went for interviews was the local social services building. This had offices for housing, health, and other services, including day care. A low, unpleasantly bureaucratic looking building, its windows were plastered with notices of tenants' rights meetings and local art exhibits. Despite its grim appearance, it serves as a vital focus for the poor of East Urban to fight for their rights against the invasion of gentrification. Marjory, whose office was in this building, had agreed to be interviewed about East Urban's government-subsidized day care centers.

Marjory struck me as a highly professional and competent career woman, liberal-minded in her strong feelings that day care services should be increased and relocated into better buildings. Since neither career women nor knowledgeability about day care centers was associated in my mind with Born and Raised East Urbanites, it did not at first occur to me that Marjory might belong to that group. A question about infant care, however, started her on an account of her own child care story.

Marjory began by saying she personally preferred to see infants in the care of parents or relatives because "that's how I had my children." She had decided to go back to work when the youngest of her three children began kindergarten. Because her own mother had held a job since the death of her husband and so was not available for child care, Marjory turned to her mother-in-law. Her mother-in-law had worked for years as a babysitter, never for more than one or two families, as a "little part-time job at home." She was able to care for Marjory's children, providing care after school, in the summer months, and during school holidays. Since Marjory's job ended at 4 p.m. and her office was only three blocks from her mother-in-law's, after-school care was required for only about an hour a day, and the children "enjoyed going to Nanny's after school."

Marjory described her mother-in-law as a "great lady" who raised six boys of her own in addition to doing babysitting for 30 years. "She was an Irish immigrant who believed in the work ethic and worked very hard all her life." Because she was separated from her husband when her children were young, she "was the exception and had to work." She first took a job assembling cardboard boxes because the factory was right across the street from her house. Her boys were on their own but were looked after by responsible neighbors, and their mother was nearby.

> It was different in those days because most mothers were not working. So everybody kind of looked out for everybody's kids—in East Urban especially because everybody knew everybody. If they had a problem, it would be nothing to knock on the next door. The neighbors would even come in and say, "What are you doing?" Everybody was everybody's mother. Especially on that block because half of them were related to each other. You were never alone.

She later began babysitting and combined this daytime work with cleaning offices at night. Marjory admires this kind of industry. "My mother-in-law was 86 when she died and was still painting her own house up until the week she passed away. She was an incredible woman. I wish I could be like her."

Marjory told me how she reached the decision to become a working mother herself.

> I was paying $125 a month rent for a four-room apartment at the time that I didn't work. When I went back to work, I was in an apartment that was $350 a month plus utilities, and it began to get a little tight. And you also want a little extra, so I went back to work. But I didn't even consider day care. I had my mother-in-law, and at the time day care centers were very new in East Urban. To put my children with a stranger wasn't something I even considered. At the time, my mother-in-law wasn't watching any other children, and the job opportunity came up. It was right in East Urban. I never intended to go back to work in the City because I thought that was too much of a hassle to come home and care for three kids. I also had a handicapped child, which I needed to be accessible for if anything happened. So the only reason I went back to work was I

had an opportunity in East Urban. I didn't think I was going to be able to do it with three children, but it worked out and I never stopped working. It's very hard to give it up.

Marjory's children are now teenagers. Since their grandmother's death, the two older girls have taken turns being responsible for their younger, handicapped brother after school. Marjory hopes that her children will be able to attend college, and that is another reason for her to provide a second income—"It goes on and on." The family is also dependent on the benefits that come with Marjory's job. Besides, she has grown used to the stimulation of outside work. "I think I'd go crazy at home now. You have nobody at home. What would you do? You can clean your house in an hour after everybody's gone. Then what do you do for the rest of the day?"

Marjory could not see herself as a babysitter for other children besides her own. "I raised three. I didn't want any more. It's a very big responsibility. Not that I don't like children. I do, but that's not my forte." Although she is looking forward to having grandchildren, she would not give up her job to stay home to babysit for them during the day. "I wouldn't do that as a job," she said. But then she added, "Of course, I would be available if they need me."

*   *   *

Marjory's mother-in-law lived on the same block as Mary O'Malley, and Marjory lives only two blocks away, but her story is a variation of Mary's. Mary had chosen to become a day care provider rather than take a job outside the home. Marjory had chosen the other path and established a career. But the attitudes of both women toward child care and work outside the home were remarkably similar.

Although Marjory eventually established a career, she did not initially think in those terms. She waited until her children were in school before looking for a job, driven primarily by the rising cost of housing. Her first considerations in the job search were hours and location, which minimized the amount of outside child care she would need. Whether she would have sought an outside job if grandmother care had not been available to her is questionable, even though she now says of herself that child care is not her forte.

Marjory's decision to work outside the home and to rely on child care, even though one of her children is handicapped, may have been influenced by the fact that both her own mother and her mother-in-law had taken outside jobs. (Marjory was a teenager when her father died and her mother took a job.) Both of these women, however, were "forced" to seek outside employment. As the sole support of their families, they were the "exceptions," mothers whose outside employment gained community approval.

Self-sufficiency—"the work ethic"—was prized, even at the cost of leaving children at home without direct adult supervision. In a previous generation these arrangements could be justified within a close-knit community of caring and responsible neighbors. And even after her mother-in-law's death Marjory decided to put her handicapped son in the care of his sisters at home rather than to seek a babysitter or professionally run after-school care for him.

A major difference between generations in Marjory's family is the kind of work these mothers found. Marjory's grandmother, a first-generation immigrant, had to take a job in a cardboard box factory in order to be near home. Not only is this kind of arrangement increasingly rare as small manufacturing concerns leave East Urban, but better opportunities are opening for Born and Raised women. Marjory was able to find a white-collar office job that led to an administrative career post. She now finds her work more stimulating than staying at home would be. She also expects that her daughters, unlike women of her own generation, will go to college. They, presumably, will also find better jobs.

Marjory assumes that the next generation will consist of two working parents because they "can't afford to live on one income anymore the way we could." She has not really thought through what her daughters will do for child care. But she is sure of one thing. She will not be available as a full-time babysitter.

TINA AND ALICIA: TURNING TO CENTER-BASED CARE

Another mother, Tina, told a different kind of story that showed what can happen when grandmothers become unavailable for child care. I had asked the director of a publicly funded day care center for the names of any Born and Raised parents whose children were in the center. She suggested I talk to Tina. When I telephoned Tina, she agreed to meet me and suggested that I might want to talk to her sister, Alicia, as well. I suspected that Tina wanted company during the interview, and I agreed to meet Tina at Alicia's apartment.

Alicia lives on a rather rundown street of East Urban's typical three-story row houses, now converted to floor-through apartments. Looking for the house number I had been given, I spotted a woman standing on her front stoop scanning the street. Sure enough, she was standing at the right number, but she gave me no sign of recognition. Correctly guessing this was Alicia, but feeling awkward, I introduced myself and asked if she was expecting me. "No," she said, "I am looking for my sister." Once again I was struck by how uneasy these women are with strangers.

When Tina finally arrived and we were all settled around Alicia's kitchen table over cups of coffee, everyone relaxed. Once Tina began her story, she talked easily and with frankness. Tina has two children, Anthony, seven, and Robby, three. Her husband works as a security guard. Tina worked as a clerk for a large corporation in the City until Anthony was born. Although she would have liked to stay home with the baby, the family depended on her income.

Tina would have preferred to have her mother care for Anthony, but her mother's health was so frail that Tina didn't want to burden her with the care of an infant. Instead, she looked for someone who might come to her house as a babysitter, but she found this to be too expensive. She then tried to find someone in her neighborhood, but the only woman who was willing to do babysitting had four young children of her own, and Tina did not want to entrust an additional infant to her. Finally, Tina turned to her ailing mother because she saw no other solution. Tina took Anthony to her mother's house every day and paid her for child care.

When Anthony was three, his grandmother's health had deteriorated to the point where she could no longer care for him. Tina's husband worked night shifts and might have been able to take on some of the daytime child care except that his schedule was irregular. With her only relative available for child care incapacitated, and with no suitable neighbors, Tina had to look to strangers for child care.

> I had heard of day cares, but I never took an interest in them, and I guess I always thought that I'd have my mother and father with me to watch the kids. I would hear a lot from women at work about their kids in day cares. I'd see them in the morning, rushing in, saying, "Oh, by the time I dropped my kids off . . ." and, "I had trouble with the day care." And I said, "I hope I don't have to do that. I hope I always have my mother and father around to watch the kids." But it doesn't always work that way.

Tina looked around for a day care center. She first put Anthony in a low-cost, licensed private center in a nearby town but took him out after only 4 days.

It looked more just like a babysiting service. There were all
these kids in one room, the TV going all day, broken toys. I'd
stay awhile and check everything out. Every day I'd pick him
up, and he'd cry and tell me he didn't like it there. If I had
wanted my son to watch TV, I would have kept him home.
He'd tell me, "We watched cartoons." He always complained to
me that the toys were all broken and so they couldn't play with
them.

Tina then remembered that she had often passed a sign right in
her own neighborhood for a publicly funded day care center. Although she knew no families who had put their children there, she
went in for an interview and was impressed when she toured the
program.

It looked like a day care. Each group was divided into age
groups, and you could see the activities. She showed me the
planning book. The teachers had their own groups of kids. Not
like the other one that had them all mixed together. I liked
what I saw. And I felt comfortable with it.

Tina waited 1 month on the waiting list before Anthony was admitted.
Because the center was subsidized, her fees were $35 a week, com-
pared with the $40 charged by the other private center where she had
gone first.

When Anthony was four, Tina had her second baby, Robby.
Because the grandmother was now far too infirm to stay with the
baby, Tina stayed home from work for 3 months. When she returned
to work she tried to put Robby in the same day care center as Anthony.
Although the center had a small infant program, there was no room for
Robby. Instead, Tina paid $80 a week for care in another private East
Urban day care center. Tina had to wait until Robby was two before a
place became available for him in the subsidized center. By this time,
Anthony had entered Catholic school and attended its after-school
program.

Tina now had her child care arrangements in place, but she ran
into problems at work. Transferred to a new section, she found that
her schedule was changed, and she was asked to start work at 8:30 in
the morning. It was impossible to drop both children off and arrive at
her office in the City on time. She asked if she could make up the time
during her lunch hour, but the company turned down her request, and
she was forced to quit her job after 14 years of work.

They're my kids, and I have the first obligation to get them off to school. I tried to explain to them that I was willing to work. I didn't want to quit. I couldn't afford to quit. I just needed that extra half an hour, which I was willing to give up a half-hour lunch for. But they wouldn't.

Tina could not find another comparable job and has had to take a job in East Urban as a drugstore cashier, working part-time, 9 a.m. to 2 p.m., at $4.25 an hour. Her center fees have been reduced to $24 a week. "We make just enough so we can make it through the month, pay our bills, and buy a little groceries," says Tina, but she will have to find full-time work by the start of the next school year in order to afford Anthony's school tuition.

Alicia, who is younger than Tina, has also had child care problems. When her daughter, Irene, was born, Alicia's husband was only sporadically employed and the family depended on her earnings. Since she was unable to use her ailing mother for child care, she turned to her mother-in-law, who lived next door and welcomed the payments Alicia made for child care. The mother-in-law subsequently moved in with Alicia and her husband and took care of Irene for 3 years. Relations became strained, however, and when Alicia's working day was lengthened by one hour her mother-in-law refused to continue child care.

At that point Alicia decided to use the same publicly funded day care center that Tina had found. Soon after that she was laid off from her job. When her second child was born, she decided to drop out of the job market to stay at home rather than put the infant in a day care center. "I think that at a younger age they need the parent more," she explained. "They need more care than the day cares could give them." Her husband, who works as a grinder in a propeller factor, now makes "enough so we can scrimp by." As long as the family can make it on his salary, her husband wants her to stay at home.

As I was about to leave, Alicia told me about a dream she had the night before. She dreamed that she had gone back to her old job and found that they had started a day care center. But she realized that her children had grown to adults and that it was too late for her. "Why do you think I dreamed that?" she asked me, and then, after a pause, answered her own question. "I guess because I was thinking about your coming."

*   *   *

Tina and Alicia are mothers who have had to work to support their families, but whose traditional child support systems of family and neighbors have failed them. Tina first heard about day care centers from her co-workers. She assumed she would never need such arrangements, but, as she says, "it doesn't always work that way."

Even though she had no East Urban friends who used day care centers, she nevertheless had definite ideas about quality. The first center was judged immediately to be unacceptable on several counts. It was shoddy and had no program besides television. Interestingly, Tina saw this as "more just like a babysitting service." She had higher expectations from center-based care. When she toured the subsidized center, "it looked like a day care." By this, Tina meant that it was more school-like, with age-segregated groups and planned activities. Tina's expectations for day care centers were that they should be more like educational settings and less like home-based babysitting.

Tina's and Alicia's stories depict a family that is growing more accepting of center-based care. Tina was the first to venture into the neighborhood day care center when Anthony was three and leaving his grandmother's care. When Tina's next child was born, she sought center-based care for her infant—a daring step for a Born and Raised mother. When Alicia's unsatisfactory child care arrangements with her mother-in-law broke down, she followed Tina's example and applied to the day care center for 3-year-old Irene. Alicia, however, unlike Tina, will not use center-based care for an infant, and since she has no alternative for her second child she has dropped out of the labor market as the only solution.

MICHELLE: BABYSITTERS AND DAY CARES

Michelle was a different kind of mother from the other Born and Raised parents I interviewed. After growing up in a family of eight children, with an abusive, alcoholic father, Michelle had established an independent life of her own. As a young teenager she had been hired as a live-in babysitter for a middle-class East Urban family. The mother in this family was a nursery school teacher who may have applied some of her professional training to the rearing of her own children. In any case, she provided for Michelle a model of a different way of rearing children than the one Michelle had grown up with.[2] Because of this experience and her own professional training as a nurse, Michelle absorbed, and adopted as her own, ways of rearing children that differed radically from those of her parents. Unlike other Born and Raised women I met, Michelle is a strong feminist and expects her husband to share fully in household duties, including child care.

Michelle works as a practical nurse in a municipal clinic, and it was through her connections there that I met her. She lives in a floor-through apartment in a building that her husband remodeled. (He is a nonunion plumber.) On the day of our interview the apartment appeared cozily cluttered, neither "picked up" for the occasion nor unduly messy. Michelle, dressed casually in shirt and pants, answered questions readily. During the interview 3-month-old Annie napped in a mechanized swing seat. Edward, a first grader, was in public school.

When Edward was 3-and-a-half-months old, Michelle's husband was out of work. Although Michelle would have liked to stay at home for a few more months with Edward, she was forced to return to full-time nursing. Neither grandmother was available for babysitting. Gentrification had forced Michelle's mother into another town, where she now holds a job, and Michelle's husband's parents had also moved away to be near their daughter and to babysit for her children.

Michelle knows all about day care centers and thinks they are fine for older children, but she prefers family day care for infants. Comfortable with strangers, she doesn't hesitate to seek babysitters beyond her immediate neighbors, but even so she has had difficulties. Lacking relatives and neighbors who were willing to care for children, she had "no prospects for a babysitter" and "just grabbed at straws, word of mouth." None of her arrangements lasted, and by the time of Edward's first birthday, Michelle had run through 10 different babysitters.

Part of the reason for such a high turnover in babysitters, Michelle admitted, was because Edward is a difficult child to care for.

> I had a very active infant. It's very few and far between that you find sitters who are into that. Because they like children who want to sit. That's my experience. If you have an infant that would sit in a seat and they could clean their house and watch the soaps and do whatever they have to do, then it might last. But I had a very active infant. He's still a pain in the ass at six. He just took a lot of energy. They'd try to put him in a playpen, and that would last about a day. I would say, "Your best bet is to go out every nice day. If you have errands to run, I don't mind him going out." And they would just say, "I'm sorry, I can't sit anymore."

Michelle felt that, ironically, taking care of Edward caused her babysitters to abandon child care in favor of a "regular job." "Why sit for the kid for $3 an hour when for minimum wage you could get a job where you can sit down all day?"

The first successful arrangement, which lasted a year, was with the mother of a 2-year-old who also cared for Edward in her home. According to Michelle, the babysitter was "loving and energetic" but her own 2-year-old was jealous and "spent the whole time pretty much beating Edward up." The following year, when Edward was two, Michelle left him with another woman who cared for three 2-year-olds, one of them her own. Her child care was "excellent," but Michelle did not like the woman's husband and thought him "weird." He appeared depressed and "pretty catatonic." (But as far as she knew, he did not bother the children.)

By the end of that year, Michelle's husband had found a job and she was able to reduce her working hours to part-time. She also felt that Edward was old enough at three to be put in a day care center. Michelle knew she was eligible for publicly subsidized child care, so she chose a bilingual subsidized center located in a Spanish-speaking church. The center would take Edward only on a 5-day-a-week basis, but even so the fee was only $50 a week, compared with the $75 she had been paying babysitters. She liked the people who ran the center but didn't like the space, which was in the church basement and repeatedly flooded due to plumbing problems.

When Edward was almost four, Michelle switched to another subsidized center in a newer building. She liked this second center. "It was great," she says. "It was clean, the teachers were nice, the food was okay. My biggest complaint about them is that they are great for 3-year-olds, but for 4-year-olds the program seems to have a dead end." Michelle feels the naps are too long for 4-year-olds and blames this on the center's giving teachers time off during the children's naps in compensation for the low pay they receive.

Michelle plans to return to part-time work. She thinks that 6 months at home with Annie is about right, and the family can make good use of a second income. Soon she will start all over again to look for another babysitter.

*   *   *

Michelle is not afraid to make child care arrangements beyond her immediate circle of relatives and neighbors. For her the issue is one of quality, judged by the principles of child development rather than of personal relationships. Her standards are high, and if she is not satisfied she finds someone else, even if that means constant changes in caregivers.

Since there is no licensed family day care in East Urban, Michelle had only her own perceptions to judge by. What she wanted for her active son was a caregiver who would channel his energy into interesting activities, such as going to the park or on errands. Michelle disapproves of babysitters who encourage passivity in children. Her ideal care is "loving and energetic." When she located such women, however, there were other problems—a jealous child, a depressed husband.

Michelle apparently has no prejudices against the children in publicly subsidized day care centers. Her first choice was a center whose population is almost totally Hispanic, and her second choice was the center with the largest black enrollment. Her criticisms are not of the kinds of families who use day care centers, but of the facilities and the program. The first basement location she considered unsafe. The second center, in her opinion, had a program that was suitable for 3-year-olds but not for 4-year-olds. Again, her standards are for developmentally appropriate practice rather than family-based values.

CHANGING PATTERNS

In these stories of Tommy, Suzanne, Marjory, Tina, Alicia, and Michelle we see parents who are grappling with changes in family patterns of child care. As these changes in child care take place, they are measured against an idealized arrangement of maternal care. When mothers, for whatever reason, are employed outside the home, they try to make arrangements that come closest to the ideal. They stay home until their children are school age. They turn to grandmothers— starting with their own mother and turning to their mother-in-law as a second choice. They will use neighbors, if available, and only as a last resort turn to care by "strangers," either in family day care or in center-based care.

But these stories also illustrate how Born and Raised parents are departing from old ways and adopting new ones. Tommy, who prides himself as a bastion of traditional Born and Raised values, has accepted the idea of his wife taking a job—not because of necessity but to improve their standard of living. Suzanne, who relied on her mother for child care within the family, put her children in Head Start for school preparation. Marjory felt she was able to take a job only because her much-admired mother-in-law was available as a babysitter. Yet Marjory herself does not plan to provide a similar service for her own grandchildren. Tina and Alicia, faced with a breakdown of grandmother care, took the audacious, for them, step of using a day care center. And Michelle, who is without nearby family, accepts care by strangers, whether as babysitters or as trained professionals in day care centers, as a matter of course.

To the extent that East Urban has remained a city where grandmothers are available to their grandchildren, where kinship networks still exist, and where well-known neighbors care for each other's children, child care arrangements can be met within these familiar boundaries. But Born and Raised families are embedded in an economic system that has resulted in family change. Old neighborhoods are broken by gentrification. Relatives are scattering. More and more women are at work, even mothers of very young children. The need for child care is increasing beyond what can be supplied by relatives and friends, and Born and Raised parents must turn to outsiders. Parents who implicitly trusted their family for proper and loving care must now find ways to adapt these old values to new patterns of child care with babysitters who are strangers and in day care centers run by professionals.

Chapter 3

Babysitters Describe Their Work

Part of my research plan was to interview women from the Born and Raised group who, like Mary O'Malley, worked as family day care providers or, as they would label themselves, babysitters. I had found that Born and Raised parents preferred Born and Raised women as babysitters, but I also knew that those women were in short supply and served professional, middle-class parents as well as their own relatives and Born and Raised neighbors. I wanted to learn more about these women who played such an important role as caregivers in East Urban.

I was eager to find out how they had decided to become caregivers, what their rates were and how fees were set, what their concerns were about the legality of their work, what their working conditions were like, what they believed were good child rearing practices, and how caring for "outsider" children affected other members of their families. Although I had decided that interviewing babysitters while they cared for children was impractical, I hoped to gain some idea of the quality of their services from their descriptions of their work.

In one way Born and Raised babysitters were easier to interview than parents. Babysitters, at least, recognized themselves as pertinent to my study. Understanding the intent of my research, they readily supplied the details of their work and suggested other babysitters I might interview. Born and Raised babysitters tended to be well established and widely known in their communities. They were proud of their work and had no trouble finding children to care for. A major difficulty, however, was that some babysitters refused to be interviewed because their work was "off the books," that is, they did not report their income for taxation. They would not trust me, as an outside interviewer, not to report them to authorities for tax evasion.

They were less concerned about their legal status in terms of regulation. The state had no licensing requirement for family day care. Instead, under a recently instigated plan, providers could voluntarily apply for Certificates of Registration through a local sponsoring organization, which would then be responsible for monitoring (at least once every 2 years) and training. Most of the Born and Raised caregivers I interviewed, however, had not yet heard of the new regulation, and those who had heard of it had no plans to register.

Providers who cared for more than five children were required by state law to become licensed as day care centers. Taking care of more than five children without a license was illegal, and all the caregivers I talked to were well aware of this limitation. However, since most took care of only a few children or, in the case of larger groups, children on staggered schedules, almost all operated legally.

I formally interviewed nine Born and Raised babysitters about their work. I talked to those who worked in their own homes as well as those who worked in the children's parents' homes. These informants gave me additional information about the work of their friends who were also babysitters. I also learned about the work of Born and Raised babysitters from the parents who were using their services.

THE WORK OF BABYSITTING

I wanted to know how babysitters got into their particular work and how it fit into their overall history of employment. I encouraged them to talk about how they made their decisions to become babysitters and what other alternatives they might have considered at that time. I also asked about how satisfied they were with their babysitting jobs.

Deciding to Become a Babysitter

In the following accounts, women describe the circumstances surrounding their decisions to become babysitters.

The first, a grandmother who has always lived in the same neighborhood, has been a babysitter for 19 years, since the youngest of her children approached school age. She recalled, "A neighbor down the block asked me if I'd watch her little one. I said fine. And ever since then my name's been getting around the neighborhood, and I've been doing it ever since." Her only other employment was as a clerk at Woolworth's the year before her first pregnancy. She says she also got into babysitting because she was lonely. She had always hoped to have five children, but because of an Rh factor had only three. She wanted more children to care for, but also wanted to be with her own children during after-school hours. Although she likes child care, she would not want to work in a day care center because there would be "too many children." She values her independence as a babysitter, explaining, "I like to do what I want to do."

Another grandmother, whose husband deserted her early in their marriage, was a waitress for 20 years, but when the restaurant went out of business she decided to try something else. She likes service jobs and a personal relationship with her employers. As a waitress she had enjoyed "meeting the public" and working for tips. "I'd never work in a factory," she says. "I'm not the kind of person to be in a factory 8 hours a day." She put an advertisement in the local paper offering to do housecleaning, and the people she cleaned for asked if she would do babysitting as well. "I started doing that," she says. "I do everything." She likes both jobs, and of babysitting she says, "The money's good—plus the kids."

A third grandmother, recently divorced from an abusive husband, began babysitting 18 years ago when the youngest of her four children was seven. Her first babysitting job was for the daughter of factory workers, a child the same age as her own daughter. She provided daily after-school care for the child, who joined her own children in play. She explained that she hasn't been a babysitter continuously. She worked at McDonald's after all her children were in school. Although she liked the job—"it kept you on the go; it was always busy"—the pay was low. She took another job, at a bank where she would get higher pay and benefits, but left after only one week because the work was "boring." Another time she interrupted her babysitting work for a year and a half to take a job as a home health aide. She liked the job, but the pay was low ($40 a week for part-time work) and she got no vacation. All in all, babysitting has been her most satisfying job. She is a person who enjoys working with people and taking care of them, but she also liked staying at home to care for her own children when they were young. "I enjoyed it," she says, "and we could make ends meet."

A younger woman, whose husband is sporadically out of work, moved to babysitting from a job as a cashier, which she took after her two children reached school age. Her cashier's job at K-Mart had been a rotating one, so that she sometimes worked Saturdays and Sundays. She learned from other babysitters what they were charging professional parents for child care and decided that as a babysitter she could earn the same pay that she earned as a cashier. Working as a babysitter would also free her weekends and allow her to take care of her own children when they came home from school. She got her first baby-sitting assignment by answering an ad for a live-in babysitter, but was able to persuade the parents to allow her to care for their infant in her own home.

Another woman who is a young mother has never had any job other than babysitting and says she has "always taken care of kids," starting as the oldest sister in a family of six children. "I was the in-house person, my mother's right-hand man. I always babysat." She started caring for children outside her own family when she was a teenager. Because she didn't finish high school she felt that other job options were limited. After her first child was born she took in another infant, whom she cared for from age 6 months to 5 years. After the birth of her second child she took no more outside children until her own youngest child was 3 years old. At that point she began to babysit in her home for several children at a time. She got her first children by putting an ad in the newspaper, and since then it's been by word of mouth. She likes her work and says, "I'm only 27, and it makes me feel young. It makes me feel good. I like the little ones—up to 4 years." She explains that she can have no more children of her own because she'd had a tubal ligation and so is glad to be able to care for children through babysitting.

Another young mother had worked as a receptionist but began babysitting after the birth of her daughter. She chose babysitting because

> I tried to think of something that I could do and bring my
> daughter with me and still be able to concentrate on her and
> whatever else I was doing at the time. And I figured if it was
> going to be anything, it would have to be child care because
> that way that would be the job. I thought about it, and I
> thought, "I really don't want to babysit," but I just couldn't fig-
> ure out any other way. And I did it.

She works in the home of the infant she cares for and takes her own child along. She also does "light housekeeping" for her employers.

Considering the Alternatives

All of these women were mothers themselves. The older ones had uniformly followed a pattern of beginning babysitting after their own children were in full-day school. Although household incomes were low, they felt they could manage on their husband's earnings until then. The younger women had started babysitting earlier, during the time when their own children were still too young for school. They still have the option of taking another kind of job when their own children start school. The youngest, the mother of an infant daughter, began babysitting because she needed a job and wanted one that would allow her to also take care of her own child. The pattern is one of women who believe in taking care of their children themselves and who become babysitters as a way to augment their husband's earnings while maintaining their roles as a mother. The exception was the ex-waitress. She is the only one who was single when her children were young, and she took a job as a waitress. It was only after her children had grown and no longer depended on her financial support that she started babysitting.

None of these women had held any jobs other than the low-paying ones where women have traditionally been employed—receptionist, clerk, cashier, waitress, and home health aide. The employment alternatives to babysitting were not attractive and were limited by the women's lack of college or other career training. Only one woman really wants to find other employment. Her plan is to continue as a babysitter while her child is very young, but to look for other employment after a year or so. Her aspirations are for a "career." "I have spent as many years as I would really like to working for an hourly wage," she says. She is thinking of "selling a product or finding out how to invest or getting into computers."

Because of their obligations to home and family, all of these babysitters wanted to work in or near their own homes. This also limited their employment opportunities. Three women worked at housecleaning in addition to babysitting. They appeared to view both jobs as extensions of their domestic roles at home and considered themselves qualified and experienced for both kinds of work because they had developed those skills as wives and mothers within their own households.

Job satisfaction was high, with some women mentioning deep emotional commitments to caring for other people's children as a substitute for additional children they were unable to bear themselves. Babysitting among the Born and Raised in East Urban is a job where the demand exceeds the supply, where specialized training is not a requirement, and where a woman can work without unduly compromising her dedication to traditional family values.

FEES

I asked babysitters what they charged and how they decided on the
fee for their services. I also wanted to know how fees were negotiated
between parents and caregivers, whether fees were increased over
time, and whether payments were calculated by the hour or by the
week.

Setting Fees

I had been told by people familiar with child care services in East
Urban that Born and Raised babysitter fees ranged from $1 to $6 an
hour for full-time care. I found this borne out by the babysitters I
interviewed, who used a variety of methods in establishing their fees.

One woman, who cares for the children of professional families,
charges everyone $5 an hour. "Everybody knows it's $5 an hour," she
says. Taking care of four children, none full-time, she earns "maybe
$300 a week." Last year she charged only $4 an hour. When she raised
the fees, nobody complained. Hearing this, her husband asked, "Why
don't you charge them $7?" But she answered, "No, I don't want to be
greedy. I couldn't do that."

The young mother who provides in-home care for an infant and
takes her own daughter along charges $5 an hour for babysitting plus
"light housekeeping." She asked for $5 because she figured that would
be what she would need to pay her bills. She usually works 25 hours a
week (because the mother is a part-time teacher) and supplements her
family's income by running a commercial office-cleaning service with
her husband.

Another babysitter charges varying amounts per hour according
to what she feels the traffic will bear. She justifies her fees by saying,
"The people I babysit or clean for, they all have a lot of money.
They've come from the City." She has worked out fees of $100 a week
for 19 hours of care (which comes to $5.26 an hour) for one child, of $5
an hour for another, of $6 an hour as a combined fee for two siblings
she cares for together, and of a combined fee of $4 an hour for two
siblings whose mother didn't want to pay more. Of the latter arrangement, she said, 'I gave it to her for $4, but I don't think it's worth it."
Overall, she usually earns about $200 a week for babysitting and
supplements this by housecleaning and by a job taking care of children
at a gym while their mothers are in an exercise class. In contrast to her
hourly babysitting fees, she earns $25 or more for an hour of house-
cleaning—$100 for one morning's work.

When another babysitter was offered the job of taking care of a child 3 years ago when he was an infant, she asked for $3.50 an hour from his professional parents. The boy's mother said she could hire someone else for $2.50, so they compromised at $3. The babysitter feels that coming down in price helped her to get the job. The boy's mother commended the babysitter for her attitude "because I seemed like I wasn't out for the money." The child's parents had originally wanted someone who would care for their son in their home and clean their apartment as well. The $3 compromise allowed the babysitter to care for the boy at her own home and elminated the housecleaning.

Later, without consulting the babysitter, the boy's parents raised the payment to $30 a day. Two years after that, again without saying anything to the babysitter, they raised her payment to $40 a day. When the father first paid her at the new rate of $200 a week, she exclaimed, "You paid me too much!" "We thought you should get more," he explained. But the following week she was cut back, without warning, to 3 days' work so that the child, now three, could attend a private day care center 2 days a week. As a result, the babysitter's weekly payment was reduced to $120.

This babysitter would like to take care of an additional child from another family, but is not sure whether that would be acceptable to her present family, even though she now works for them only 3 days a week. Her own family finances are tight. Her husband earns only $12,000 to $14,000 a year. She "manages" three buildings in exchange for rent, and her husband does some plumbing "on the side" to make ends meet.

Another woman, whose present job is providing in-home care for a 14-week-old boy whose parents are both lawyers, works for the family 3-and-a-half days as a babysitter and a fourth day as a house-cleaner (although she also does some cleaning during the rest of the week). During the day of cleaning, the child's mother, who works only part-time, takes care of her son. The babysitter began by charging $5 an hour for babysitting and $10 an hour for housecleaning. She now earns between $240 and $260 a week for a minimum of 35 hours of combined child care and housework.

She is not sure how that works out by the hour but guesses that she's been given a raise for her babysitting hours. She has no formal arrangement for overtime although she is paid by the hour and says of her employer, "She always gives me extra. Just last week we were arguing about the money." The "argument," as the babysitter explained it, was that she was protesting that she was being overpaid. She is proud that her employer "thinks she's underpaying me and that

I'm worth more." When I asked if she considered herself worth more, she answered, "No, they are nice people, and I'm comfortable here."

Over the years this babysitter has progressively raised her fees. Since she started with parents whose pay was lower, her fees have gone up not only with time but also in response to parental earnings. "Professional people can pay more than factory people" is how she explains it. She recently heard that some East Urban professional parents are hiring babysitters from the City, Jamaicans who charge $6 an hour, the highest fees she'd heard of. She thinks this must be for housework as well as babysitting because she can't imagine that black women could command those fees for babysitting alone.

Another babysitter, who works for working-class parents with such jobs as deliveryman, truck driver, restaurant worker, and factory seamstress, charges everyone $3 an hour except the parents of her friend's grandchild, whom she charges only $2 an hour "as a favor to the family" and because she "knows they need money." In explaining her low rates, she says, "If it was me, and I was trying to help myself out, I'd want to afford it." She says she wants "to help out" when families face "these high prices." She makes the point that she's not in business for the money.

Another woman, a single parent, who also cares for children whose parents have low-income jobs, varies her fees according to what she judges parents can pay. She charges $3 an hour for one child whom she cares for 2 days a week. She charges $4 an hour for another child who stays with her 6 evenings a week. For another child, who stays 2 nights a week, she charges $4 an hour. She also cares for her niece and nephew every night from 7:30 p.m. to 7:30 a.m. for a combined fee of only $80 a week—a lower rate because they are relatives. By taking care of five children on different schedules, she is able to make about $350 a week.

Babysitters charged fees according to household income, but there was considerable variation within each category. Fees were negotiated within a rather broad spectrum ranging from $3 to $5.50 an hour for children of professional parents, to $1 to $3 an hour for children of lower-income parents. It is customary to charge less for siblings, regardless of the income of parents. Since this family day care was not subsidized by government funding, babysitters, in effect, subsidized fees by charging less to needy families. Professional parents also paid relatively low fees, when considered as a percentage of two-career earnings. These parents were willing and able to pay much higher rates for housecleaning than for child care.

Hourly or Weekly Payments

Babysitters who worked for lower-income families were paid by the hour. Those who worked for professional families were paid either by the hour or by the week, but some babysitters appeared to be uncomfortable with weekly payments and said they preferred to be paid by the hour. They feared that weekly payments might lead to their having to work extra hours without extra pay, but they were also uneasy about the possibility of being paid for hours they might not have actually worked. One said, for example, that she asked to be paid by the hour so she would not be "overpaid" when parents skipped a day or required fewer hours of care. Another babysitter expressed a similar sentiment when she said, "I want to get paid for what I work" (the implication being, not for unworked hours).

Most of the women I interviewed did at least some night baby-sitting, for which they charged by the hour and at reduced rates if the children slept. Higher-income parents hired babysitters for night work when the parents went out for social occasions. Low-income parents required child care to accommodate night shift working hours, and this care was sometimes overnight in the caretakers' homes.

Negotiating Fees

The women who worked for professional families had varying attitudes toward the amounts they received in fees. One who worked for professional parents bargained as best she could for higher fees, with the justification that her employers "have a lot of money." Another, by contrast, was proud that her employers, both lawyers, considered her "underpaid." She did not want to be seen as money-minded, nor did she want to view her employers as in any way exploitative. Instead, caregiver and parents operated within an arena of mutual appreciation of "niceness."

Although good babysitters are considered by professional East Urban mothers to be in short supply, parents appeared in these accounts to have considerable negotiating power in setting the terms of employment. In two instances they were able to bargain and reduce the babysitter's asking fees. Once babysitters began work, parents usually determined when and if raises should be given. Professional parents criticized babysitters who were overtly concerned with raising their fees for putting money before devotion to child care, an attitude that worked in parents' favor in setting fees.

Babysitters who worked for low-income parents set rates according to what they judged to be fair in light of parental earnings. These babysitters were the ones who saw themselves as "helpers" to families having a tough financial time. But even babysitters working for high-income families put themselves at a disadvantage when they insisted on being paid only for hours worked as a way of displaying "fairness" toward the families that employed them.

Benefits

None of the babysitters interviewed received social security or health benefits from their employers. Most received no payment when their employers decided to keep their children at home or for holidays and vacations. The exceptions were those babysitters who cared mainly for children from one professional family. These babysitters arranged to take their vacations at the same time as the family and were paid for that time.

One babysitter, who had always been paid by the hour and had worked as a babysitter for many years, was finally beginning to reconsider her position of not being paid when her employers took days off and didn't need her services. "Maybe I'm going to have to put my foot down and say, 'If you're off that has nothing to do with me. If I'm off sick, fine.' But," she added with a laugh, "I never admit I'm sick."

Although babysitters receive almost none of the benefits ordinarily accorded to employees, they accept these arrangements without overt protest. They view themselves as self-sacrificing, caring individuals who prefer to endure hard working conditions and low pay rather than to make demands of the families they serve.

QUESTIONS OF LEGALITY

Group Size and Licensing

The numbers of children cared for by the babysitters I formally interviewed ranged from one to eight, the latter in addition to the babysitter's own two children, but not all at once. (In figuring the maximum number of children that can be cared for without a day care center license, the state excludes one's own children and those for whom no fee is charged, but caring for more than eight children at any one time is illegal in any case.) Although few people had heard of the recent plan of voluntary registration of family day care providers, the one regulation that all babysitters quoted to me was that caring for more than five children for a fee is illegal.

Babysitters who cared for children of low-income parents cared for more children than those who cared for children of high-income parents. The only babysitters I heard about in East Urban who were caring for more than the legal number of five children were caring for children whose parents were low-income. Since fees charged to low-income parents were lower, babysitters who worked for low-income parents had to accept larger numbers of children to generate more income. It is also likely that professional parents do not use babysitters who care for large groups of children. When I interviewed professional parents, they said they strongly preferred in-home babysitters or those who would care for their own children exclusively.

Babysitters caring for the children of professionals preferred to take a child from infancy (usually between 6 weeks and 3 months) until the child entered preschool. Since career mothers were apt to go back to their jobs when their children were infants, babysitters could then build an ongoing and steady relationship with one family. Because it is customary to charge less for an additional sibling than for the first child, one child each from different families is most profitable for the babysitter, but babysitters working for professional parents seldom care for more than two children at one time.

Babysitters who cared for larger numbers of children from lower-earning parents accommodated to diverse work schedules. These parents were more apt to work irregular shifts than were salaried professionals whose work was basically from 9 to 5 (but often required staying late). This meant that even if babysitters of low-paying parents took care of a larger number of children, the group size at any one time might not be more than three or four.

One woman, for example, caring for five children of low-income parents in addition to her own two children, had the following schedule of children:

> an 18-month-old, 5 days, 8:30 a.m. to 1:00 p.m.,
> a 1-year-old, 6 nights, 6:00 p.m. to 10:00 p.m.,
> a 2-year-old, 2 evenings, 5:00 p.m. to 10:00 p.m.,
> and two children, five and seven, 5 full nights a week.

In general, babysitters preferred to care for no more than a few children and considered groups larger than the legal size unfeasible. One, who had just started caring for her own infant and one other child, when asked if she might take more children, answered:

Well, I don't know if I would want to do that. Because it's a very, very hard job. You know, people don't realize how hard it can be sometimes. And I think for myself I'm just not the type of person that can take care of a lot of kids. Right now anyway. I mean if I had a lot of experience I would think about it, but I don't know if it's a good idea for now. It takes a lot of patience.

When asked about group size, another babysitter said that she had heard of only one woman who cared for more than five children—a babysitter who took seven. When I asked if she herself would consider taking a large group, she quickly replied, "It's totally out of the question." She explained, "You couldn't go to the park. I'd take an infant and two toddlers or three toddlers. But you can't do two infants. There aren't enough hands." Even though people knock at her door seeking after-school care, she won't take more children.

Only one woman appeared undaunted by larger numbers of children. She had once cared for seven. Although they were "mostly at different times," she sometimes took six together at once—one 14-month-old, three 16-month-olds, and two 2-year-olds. "It was so much fun," she recalled enthusiastically. "They were all so good."

No charges of illegal numbers of children have been brought against any babysitters in East Urban, so prosecution poses no apparent threat. Even so, these babysitters appeared to have stayed, on the whole, within the law for reasons other than group size restrictions. Because their services are in demand, they could have increased the number of children they cared for. What limited group size was parent preference and the babysitters' assessments of their own limitations.

Reporting Income

Although babysitters, for reasons of their own, mostly stayed within legal limits of group size, they were not so law-abiding when it came to reporting their income for tax purposes. Few of the babysitters interviewed paid taxes on their earnings, and it was commonly assumed that all East Urban babysitting was "off the books" as a source of income. Some babysitters asked to be paid in cash, thinking that would protect them from government tracking. Others were willing to accept checks but assumed they would not be prosecuted.

The babysitters did not know whether their employers used the dependent care tax credit (which allows employed parents to deduct a portion of their child care expenses from their federal taxes), but none had been asked to supply their employers with social security numbers. Nor would they have wanted to, for tax reasons. The general attitude among Born and Raised babysitters toward evading taxes was that "what you do is your business, what I do is mine."

Since their earnings were low, babysitters felt they could not afford to pay taxes. As one explained, "I don't want to work that I have to pay taxes. It's not worth it." Another said that she had been on public assistance after her husband moved out and that her babysitting earnings had enabled her eventually to leave the welfare rolls. Even so, she did not report her child care income. Instead, she claimed that she was receiving financial support from another member of her household.

Another woman said of her employers, who are professionals, "They never said nothing, so I never. I get paid by cash. No checks." When asked whether that meant that her employers did not claim their child care expenses as a tax credit, she answered, "They probably connive it some other way. If you're in business, you probably can. Not that I care."

In not reporting their income, babysitters followed the community custom of transacting informal business between individuals on a nonreporting, cash basis. At the root of these practices is a deep-seated resentment of government interference into what are considered private matters. Consequently, it is impossible to tell how reporting of income would affect these babysitters' incomes. We could assume that with their low general household income plus the business deductions they would be able to claim they would have negligible taxes on their earnings or none, at all. But this is not the way babysitters view their situation. Their view is that if they were subject to taxes, babysitting would not be "worth it." To them babysitting is viable as work only if it is untaxed.

WORKING CONDITIONS

In Whose Home?

When babysitters described their work, they talked about deciding whether to work in their own home or in the home of children's parents. Those who cared for children from only one family worked either in their own home or in the home of the children's parents. Babysitters who cared for children from more than one family worked in their own home.

Babysitters who worked in their own home gave various reasons for preferring this arrangement. Those who have children still living at home wanted to combine babysitting with caring for their own children—either full-time care for their preschool children, after-school care for their school-age children, or preparing meals for their grown children. They also wanted to combine their babysitting with caring for their husbands and dependent parents. Two women I interviewed took care of their mothers every day, bringing them to their own home and looking after them during time that partially overlapped with time spent babysitting.

Another reason babysitters gave for preferring to work in their own home was that they could do their own housekeeping as well as babysitting. They resisted having to lower their high housekeeping standards because of babysitting duties. The older women especially prided themselves on their spotless houses. A traditional Born and Raised housekeeper in East Urban may dust, vacuum, and scrub floors every day in addition to doing the cooking and laundry. One woman complained that she was no longer able to wash her curtains every month because of babysitting duties and now had to make do with only twice a year.

When these women become babysitters they try somehow to combine child care with their usual large amount of housework. One gets up at 4 or 5 a.m. and does her housework before babysitting. Others try to accomplish as much as they can before it's time to take the children to the park, or they houseclean during naptime. The only serious injury reported to me that occurred during babysitting was not to a child but to a babysitter. While she was vacuuming her carpeted stairs, the machine toppled down on top of her, gashing her head. Luckily, she was able to find a neighbor who could care for the children while she walked to the nearest hospital for treatment.

Born and Raised parents look for a clean house as a sign of quality care. The parents I talked to praised their babysitters by saying that you would never know from the appearance of the house that children had been there. For these parents a house that showed no evidence of child activity was the house of a person with high standards of cleanliness and was a safe, healthy place to leave children.

Doing housework for one's own family is very different, however, from doing it for other people's families. When babysitters work in parents' homes, they are usually expected to do at least "light housework" as well as child care. But doing professional housework is considered a lower-status job than babysitting, even though middle-class parents value Born and Raised women for their housekeeping skills and pay them at much higher rates for cleaning than for babysitting. One babysitter, in describing a friend who does babysitting, laundry, and housework in the home of two lawyers, commented disapprovingly, "She's like a maid. I don't want that." She valued her independent status in her own home over being a type of servant in someone else's home, no matter how well paid.[1]

Those babysitters who cared for children in the parents' homes did so at the parents' request, and these were all professional parents. Babysitters usually provided their own transportation, although they might be given a ride home if they had to stay later than usual. Most babysitters, however, live within a few blocks of the parents' homes where they babysit. Babysitters resist staying late if they have family obligations such as making dinner, but one babysitter takes the child to her own home if the parents are delayed.

A beginning babysitter, who placed an ad in the paper to do in-home child care and now has such a job, says she doesn't care whether she works in her own home or not. She thinks that it might be "more comfortable" to work in her own home but that it's "good to get out to work and then have your home to yourself."

Although the pattern in general is to do one kind of babysitting or another, either in the parents' home or in the caregiver's, some women do both. One woman, who had cared for children in her own home for many years, was recently persuaded to take care of an infant in the parents' home on the promise that when the baby grew older she might take him to her house. She has mixed feelings about the arrangement. On the one hand, "there are many things I'd like to do at home," she says, mentioning housecleaning tasks in particular. On the other hand, she says with obvious surprise, "I find I enjoy being here so much. It's like a break from my house. It's relaxing."

In their own homes women are better able to combine babysitting with their traditional roles as nurturing mothers and capable house-keepers. They take pride in their abilities and skills and do not want to be forced to lower their high standards because of babysitting work. Although it is career women who are often described as wanting to "have it all" when they aspire to be ideal wives, mothers, and execu-tives, these women who work as babysitters also try to "have it all" by maintaining their traditional roles while taking on the extra responsibil-ities of babysitting.

Babysitters who work in the homes of parents face problems of double responsibilities to two families—their own and their employ-ers'. Unlike "au pairs," young women who have no family responsibili-ties of their own, the Born and Raised babysitters must meet their employers' demands while maintaining their own family obligations.

Although going out to work has some compensations, such as "getting away" from home, these babysitters are women who prefer traditional women's work to "outside" employment and would, in the main, prefer to stay in their own homes.

Loneliness

Whether babysitters work in their own homes or in parents' homes, they run the hazard of loneliness from lack of contact with other adults. My impression was that babysitters spend a good deal of their time on the telephone talking to relatives and friends. During interviews the telephone was apt to ring repeatedly, and obviously familiar callers would be told to call back later. One babysitter told me how she had attached a 150-foot cord to her telephone so that she could talk to her sister daily and care for children at the same time. Telephones were usually in the kitchen, so that it was possible to telephone and supervise children or perform household tasks at the same time.

Parks, where babysitters take children to be outdoors, provide a place to talk to other babysitters, friends, or relatives. Sometimes when I wanted to reach a babysitter I had been unable to contact by telephone, I would go to the park where I knew she made daily visits and find her there. Outings to shop or run errands provide additional relief from being housebound. "I don't like to be cooped in the house," explained a babysitter who takes her charges to McDonalds if the weather is too bad for a park visit.

Unlike other jobs, which might place restrictions on talk with relatives and friends, the job of babysitting allows workers to keep daily contacts by telephoning and visiting in the park. Nevertheless, loneliness can be a problem, particularly when the weather is bad. If these babysitters had voluntarily registered as family day care providers with authorized sponsoring organizations, they might have developed networks of colleagues, but none spoke of their lack of professional ties.

Stress

We might expect that caring for several young children would be arduous, but only one babysitter talked to me directly about stress. She described how she takes a bubble bath after the last child leaves and tells herself, "Don't worry. Calm down." She consoles herself by comparing her child care burden, where children at least go home at the end of the day, with the responsibilities her mother had in caring for six of her own children round the clock. Since most of the Born and Raised babysitters I talked to come from large families themselves, they may not think caring for a number of children is in itself a particularly stressful situation. If this is the case, younger babysitters, coming from smaller families and with shrinking kinship networks, may not be so experienced at caring for several children at once.

CHILD REARING

Babysitters recognize the role of parents in setting standards for the care of their children. "They want it a certain way and you can't argue with them," explained one. At the same time, babysitters believe that the best care they can give children is to treat them as their own. One of the advantages of being a mother as well as a babysitter, as they see it, is to try as much as possible to apply the same standards in the care of "outside" children that they have to their own children.

None of the babysitters I interviewed had received any kind of formal training except those who had worked in day care centers or Head Start. This may in part reflect the absence of family day care licensing in East Urban. Kisker, Maynard, Gordon, and Strain (1988), in a large-scale survey of family day care providers, found that more than one-third reported that they had received some specific child care training, most often courses in child development or early education, and that licensed family providers were much more likely than unlicensed providers to have had some training.

"Good" Care

When babysitters talk about what is important to them in caring for children, they emphasize physical care—keeping children safe, clean, and well fed. One woman who cares for a toddler answered the question of what was important as a babysitter by saying:

> To take care of them physically. Know when they need to be changed and fed. Take care of basic needs. And also to be able to give a little bit to them emotionally. To play with them and make them smile. I don't know how much one person who is not their parent can really give to them. You know, I don't really think there is that much that's required. A lot of patience. I think that's one thing that you definitely have to have. If they start to cry, if one thing doesn't work, try another.

Children were judged by how "good" they were. Praise for children included, "She's so sweet, she's really a good little girl" and "Basically, they are all good." Babysitters indicated that being "good" means being compliant and not resisting authority. Sometimes children were given rewards—candy or a small gift—for good behavior. Mothers were also praised for being "nice" and "sweet."

I had planned no formal observations of how babysitters behaved with the children in their care and observed only casually when children happened to be present during my interviews. I gained some information about the quality of care, however, from babysitters' accounts. For example, one babysitter reported several instances of children's "bad" behavior. She appeared to be at a loss as to how to handle children who were having difficulties.

> I have a kid now who is badly behaved, but he's only 8 months old. He does nothing but cry and cry. What are you going to do? I try to talk to him, I give him toys to play with. And the minute you pick him up and start talking to him, he stops. But I can't just hold him. He's a big kid. And then I can't take care of someone else.

The same woman reported about another child, "The kid drove me crazy. He constantly cried. He tried to put his own coat on and run out the door. 'Mommy, Mommy, I want Mommy!' I had to lock the door twice."

Another woman who did occasional after-school babysitting described how little boys who deliberately made loud burping noises embarrassed her and then added, "Sometimes they're just obnoxious little brats, and I'm not in the mood to deal with it." She concluded by saying that babysitting was probably not the job for her.

In describing children's behavior as either "good" or "bad," babysitters did not speculate on why children behaved as they did. Rather than analyzing the incidents that led to an outburst of "bad" behavior (as professionally trained caregivers are taught to do), they viewed children as acting out on the basis of their temperament. Babysitters did not think about how they might change their own patterns of behavior to affect children in more positive ways. If children were "bad," there was nothing much to be done but endure the situation. Babysitters considered themselves lucky when they got "good" children, unlucky when they got "bad" ones.

Similarly, babysitters regarded their own behavior as an outgrowth of their temperament rather than of acquired techniques. Most said that they felt they were suited to their work, by which they meant they were more tolerant than confrontational when children were difficult and were more accepting than rejecting of children's ways. One, who described herself as "very tolerant," said that parents have remarked, "God bless you and your patience." To illustrate her attitude she asked herself aloud, "Children, what trouble can they be? What's the worst they can do?" The only answer she could come up with was that they might annoy her downstairs neighbors by running.

"Healthy" Care

Born and Raised parents have strong opinions not only about what makes a "good" child but also about what makes a healthy one. They extol the healthful properties of fresh air and criticize parents from other cultural backgrounds who keep their children indoors. A babysitter says of a Filipino child in her care, who appears to her to be withdrawn, "I think he needs fresh air." Since they seldom have access to yards, which in any case are tiny, babysitters use the three city parks for getting children outdoors.

Born and Raised babysitters try to take their children to the park every day—some even when it's raining. One told me with pride, "I'm out in all kinds of weather. And I tell the mothers of all the kids I babysit, 'Give me umbrellas, raincoats.' I'll put them in plastic bags if I have to. And these kids are very seldom sick."

Even when babysitters care for several children at one time, they take them to the park. One explained that she was able to take five at once by having them hold each other's hands. She herself held the hands of those she "didn't trust." When they reached the park they dropped hands and the children ran off to play. "Sometimes I'd have to yell at them," she said, as though that was unusual. She said she warned parents that their children might have small accidents, such as scraped knees, because of being allowed to move about freely, but the parents were willing to run this risk. Babysitters talked about the healthful properties of fresh air, but it was obvious from their accounts that going to the park also provided children with the benefits of active and exploratory play.

Communicating with Parents

Babysitters reported that they had very little discussion with parents about their children's day once the initial period of employment was past. "You come, you go, you do your job," commented one. Only once did a mother telephone during my interviews. She called to say she would be late and also asked about her infant. The babysitter reported that the child was "happy and smiley" and had just gone down for a nap. At another babysitter's house I observed a mother picking up her toddler. When she asked how her daughter's day had gone, the babysitter answered, "She was really good. She ate good too." She added, "She had a little nap and slept for about half an hour."

Aside from reporting on illnesses or small accidents, communication between caregivers and parents appeared to revolve around a narrow spectrum of reporting how children ate and slept and whether they were "good." If these babysitters had been trained in a more professional way of describing children's development and activities, they might have expanded their reporting to give a more detailed picture of the children's day. As it was, the reporting served to reassure parents that babysitters had been attentive to their children.

Daily Activities

I asked babysitters about their daily schedule and what they did with the children. One described her day with two 2-year-olds and two 4-year-olds. She gets up at 6:00 in the morning and does her washing and dusting before the children arrive. When the first child comes, she "runs to a lot of stores" with him before the others come so she can take them right to the park. The children come back for lunch, play for half an hour, and then go to the park again for 2 hours. The 2-year-olds nap in a twin carriage during afternoon park time. Around 3:30 they all come back home to cookies, juice, television, and playing with toys. "They relax because they're tired."

Another babysitter also told me her rules for indoor behavior. She spreads a blanket on the living room floor to define the space where the children are allowed to play and watch television. The children even eat on the blanket, which can then be shaken out to get rid of the crumbs. "They don't walk around with cookies or anything. They're good. I say, 'if you walk around, I'm going to get ants.'" The children are not supposed to leave the living room or to sit on the living room couch. No rough play is allowed indoors. The 2-year-olds play together, and the 4-year-olds play together, with separate toys that are kept apart. Most of the toys came from the babysitter's own children who are now grown, but children can bring toys from home if they take them back at the end of the day. "And they're happy," she adds proudly. "No troubles."

This woman was clearly dedicated to keeping a neat house even at the expense of curtailing the activities of the children. But her rules were not that much out of line with what I gathered was general practice. Another babysitter described children eating on the kitchen floor because they "messed things up and pulled on the tablecloth." Another required a 3-year-old to play with his toy models on a piece of paper to protect the rug. Except for free play in the parks, it seemed that children were closely controlled so that they would not mess up carefully kept homes.

The apartments of Born and Raised families are often full floors in aging row houses or tenements. A common room arrangement is to put the kitchen, where the family also eats, in the largest room at the rear and the main bedroom at the front with windows overlooking the street, and to use the one or two small windowless intervening rooms as combination bedrooms and living rooms.

When child care is in the babysitter's home, the usual arrangement of space is to use the kitchen and adjoining living room for children's activities. Children can play games or do projects at the kitchen table or watch television and play with toys in the living room. At the end of the day, toys and any equipment are picked up and stored because this is space shared with the family. Living rooms have multiple uses—for babysitting during the day, for family relaxation after school hours and in the evening, and for sleeping on foldout couches at night. With arrangements of this sort, it is important to women to keep things orderly and in place so that living spaces can be adapted to different family purposes.

Babysitters described their activities with children as "playing" rather than "teaching." They mentioned children's activities such as coloring, board games, puzzles, train sets, modeling clay, and play with model dinosaurs. Children are not included in household activities such as cooking or cleaning. Nor are children allowed to experiment with household objects in general use, such as kitchen utensils, but are confined to child-designated toys and games. No one described active roughhousing or romping or even exercises that could be peformed indoors. Instead, indoor activities are confined to eating, napping, television, or playing with games and toys.

Any "teaching," according to babysitters, comes from television, especially *Sesame Street*. Television is an obvious help in keeping children engaged. One woman said she often turned on the same program twice as it appeared at different times on different channels, and the children enjoyed watching both times. Babysitters said they restricted television to children's programs during the day, but when their own family members came home, children watched any programs that the rest of the family wanted to see.

It appeared from babysitters' accounts of daily schedules and children's activities that children in care are kept well fed, clean, and safe. However, caring for several children in small rooms that are shared with family and where orderliness is prized places restrictions on children's activities. Except for going to the park, where children are permitted to move about more freely, children in care appear to get very little exercise.

I heard no accounts of babysitters encouraging or even taking note of dramatic and imaginative play, fantasy, storytelling, or other expressive forms of activity. Children were not encouraged to draw or paint freely, or to dance or sing (except occasionally with older children and in response to television programs). No babysitter mentioned regular reading or book-centered activities. I was given the impression that Born and Raised mothers did not raise their own children with these activities, so there was no reason to expect they would behave any differently with the children they cared for.

Attitudes Toward Parents

The babysitters I interviewed were strong believers that, ideally, mothers should stay at home with their own children. This was one of the main reasons they had taken on babysitting as a job. Consequently, their feelings toward the mothers they worked for were ambivalent, especially toward those mothers who appeared to them to work by choice rather than necessity. One babysitter expressed this ambivalence toward the career mothers she worked for by explaining, "I say I don't care what people do. I say what's the difference? They're paying me. As long as she pays me, I don't care. My girlfriends get annoyed. They'll say, 'How can she just leave her child?' I say, 'That's their thing.'" Then she added pointedly, "Of course, *we* never did that."

Others were more unequivocally opposed to the behavior of the career mothers who employed them. One commented:

> That's why at first I really didn't want to do child care, because
> I thought they should be with their child. I think that this so-
> ciety really has too many women working. Women should be
> staying home with their kids. I'm not saying that I'm telling
> them what they should do. But I think it's important not to have
> a society where kids are brought up by the babysitter. And

that's happening much too often. So they have these women who have these careers, and they don't want to give them up. And so they continue to work, and they spend a month with the child, maybe two months, and they go back to a 40- or 50- hour week. That's just not right.

According to the babysitters' own families' traditions, young mothers work only when they consider it a necessity. This results in a double standard of behavior between women within the caregivers' families and community and the outside women who are their employers. Whereas babysitters view staying at home with young children as ideal behavior for young mothers and therefore self-fulfilling, their upper-middle-class employers regard combining motherhood with a career as self-fulfilling.

OTHER FAMILY MEMBERS

When I talked to babysitters about their own family members, they discussed more readily problems between their husbands and themselves arising from babysitting arrangements than problems resulting from having their own children around when they babysat. It may be that they were reluctant to consider possible adverse consequences to their own children, since it was usually for the sake of the children that the work had been undertaken in the first place.

Husbands

Some women said their husbands regarded the outside children as though they were part of the family. "He likes having the boys around because we never had a son of our own," said one. "The two boys are so nice that my husband feels like they're his grandchildren," said another.

Other women said their husbands resented the commotion of child care. Two said that when their husbands came home from work and wanted peace and quiet away from the children, they went to their mother's apartment (which in each case was in the same building) to escape. Another said her husband went into the bedroom and shut the door to be by himself.

One woman described her husband as abusive to her and her children. His idea of discipline for children, she said, was "go slap them in the face." When I asked her how he behaved toward the child she babysat for, she said, "It's different, your kids and someone else's. You can't do what you want with other people's children."

Babysitters also described their husbands as putting up with baby-sitting activities as a trade-off for their wives staying at home. "He'll go along with it," said one, "because it keeps me home." One older woman was especially protective of her husband's feelings about her work. "I keep up my house every day," she said. "I don't want my husband saying to me, 'If this babysitting is going to interfere with your work here, then stop it.' So I try not to."

Ironically, this same woman concealed from her husband, a retired janitor with no pension, how useful her income was to their household support. She regards the $300 a week she makes from babysitting as "my money," but explains:

> He never asks me what I do with my money. But, say, a tele-phone bill was a little higher than normal. I would put that money in there. And the mortgage went up. I never told him. I put my extra money in there. It might be like $75 a month. He gives me money every week. So much for food and so much for my budget. We call it a budget. But I never said to him, "This went up $50. This went up." Being I have it, I do it. And if I don't work someday, I'll have to say, "Frankie, you have to give me a little more money." But now I try to help him.

Husbands were clearly regarded as possible barriers to the work. These women appeared to see themselves as working on sufferance, and with their husband's disapproval a constant factor to be reckoned with, although I heard of no husbands calling a halt to babysitting activities.

Children and Grandchildren

Those babysitters who were grandmothers had sometimes, like Mary O'Malley, been able to take care of both "outside" children and their own grandchildren. One, for example, was able to care for her grandchildren in their home from 8:00 a.m. to 12:30 p.m., when the children's father, who worked a night shift, could take over until their mother returned from work at 4:30 p.m. This schedule allowed the grandmother to babysit for other children in the afternoons and evenings.

Others found that their babysitting for outsiders prevented them from also caring for their grandchildren. One grandmother would not help her daughter-in-law, a factory worker, because of her hours, which interfered with babysitting for another family. The grandmother, who was single and depended on her babysitting income, refused to give up the more lucrative work. She told her daughter-in-law, "I'm not going to lose out on $100 a week to babysit for you so that you can make all the money." (Her son had offered to pay her only $40 a week.) She complained, "If you babysit for your relatives, they don't pay you nothing of what you think you should get, because you're related to them." Another grandmother, who babysits in a middle-class home and whose daughter-in-law is pregnant, said she is not interested in becoming a babysitter for her grandchild. "I don't want any more kids in the house messing it up," she says. "Now my house is clean." (Both of these cases, notably, involved daughters-in-law rather than daughters).

Since most of the babysitters I interviewed cared for outside children, care of children within their own families became more difficult. They not only faced constraints of time and competing responsibilities, but they and other family members had problems reconciling fees paid by parents outside the family with those paid by family members.[2]

BABYSITTING AS NURTURING

My interviews with babysitters from the Born and Raised community showed areas of strong commonality. All these women were mothers whose work as babysitters was heavily influenced by their commitment to their traditional family roles. As wives and mothers, they aspired to ideal models of nurturing, devoted, hard-working womanhood. These ideals carried over into their jobs as caregivers and affected all aspects of their work.

These women intially chose the work of babysitting as an extension of their role as mothers. Becoming a babysitter was not so much an ambition as an accommodation to conflicting pressures from economic necessity and family. Babysitting was viewed as a solution to the problem of earning money while at the same time staying true to their commitments to what they considered ideal behavior.

Because they liked to think of themselves as women who cared for children as an extension of their mothering role, they were willing to work for low fees, partly as proof that their motivation was love of children rather than earning money. When they worked for affluent parents, they were reluctant to ask for raises and preferred to let their employers decide when and if fees should be increased. By leaving these decisions up to the employer, babysitters were made to feel that increases were a result of devoted care rather than of a business transaction.

When they worked for lower-income parents, babysitters charged less, expressing empathy for the parents and identifying with them in a spirit of solidarity. They were reluctant to add to the difficulties of young, hard-pressed families by charging higher fees, even when the result was having to take care of larger numbers of children to produce a sufficient income for themselves. Babysitters were more comfortable in the role of a helping hand, supporting others, even at their own expense, than in the role of a businessperson calculating reasonable fees to be charged to clients.

Although Born and Raised women pride themselves on being law-abiding and ally themselves with the forces of law and order, babysitters do not report their earnings as income to be taxed. Although their actions, in this case, seem inconsistent with their beliefs, in fact they are following traditional community customs. Antagonistic to what they consider bureaucratic government intrusions into family life, the Born and Raised community takes it for granted that privately arranged transactions will be "off the books." Since babysitting is viewed as a service negotiated between private parties, it falls within the category of activities commonly accepted as not being subject to taxes. This view tends to make babysitting appear less a business transaction and more a favor offered to friends or a personal service offered to those who need it. Because they do not report their income, babysitters are ineligible for government-supported benefits such as social security and federal unemployment insurance. This reinforces babysitters' views of their work as different from regular employment.

As long as babysitters, such as those in the Born and Raised group, see themselves in traditional women's roles, they will continue to subsidize services by keeping fees low. This works to parents' advantage and lessens the burden on government funding. But younger women, with different ideas of what women's work should be, may not be so willing to sacrifice themselves for other people's children. They may become more businesslike or they may avoid babysitting altogether.

QUALITY OF CARE

Babysitters do not discuss their care of children in terms of child rearing practices. Whether children are "good" or "bad" appears to them to be a given. What they are responsible for, in their eyes, is the safety and health of the children. To this end they set high standards in such areas as cleanliness, protecting children from accidentally hurting themselves, getting children into the outdoors, and making sure they are all well fed.

When babysitters take care of either their own relatives or the children of other Born and Raised families, they work within family traditions and community-accepted norms of child rearing practices. What these children in care experience at home with their parents is congruent with what they experience with their babysitters. This is not the case when Born and Raised babysitters take care of the children of "American" parents who were themselves raised in middle-class families. American middle-class child rearing practices often differ from those of the working class. Middle-class mothers, for example, are more apt to emphasize children's self-direction; working-class mothers, children's conformity to external standards of "good" behavior.[3]

Middle-class mothers tend to ignore these differences in child rearing. They say they value their working-class babysitters for the affection they display toward the children they care for. This places the emphasis on affective or "familial" behavior rather than on "teaching" behavior. Middle-class parents will themselves assume the teaching role with their children, taking responsibility for their children's language usage and orientation to books.[4]

Since both parents and caregivers see babysitting as primarily custodial, there is little discussion with the parents about the children except for reporting of daily routines such as naps and meals. Behavior is described only in the most general terms of "happy" or "good." By circumscribing the babysitter's role to one of an affectionate custodian, mothers and caregivers can avoid areas of potential conflict—cultural conflict in the case of class differences, and conflicts about establishing authority over the child. Such distancing minimizes friction between the mothers who have chosen babysitting as their work and mothers who have chosen other, less family-oriented jobs.

In these babysitting arrangements, middle-class parents choose Born and Raised caregivers for quality custodial care offered by women whose community values—with their high priority on mothering skills—middle-class parents respect. They count on themselves as parents to provide school-oriented "teaching," and they customarily send their children to private preschools to supplement child care by babysitters. By contrast, Born and Raised parents choose babysitters from their own group. They trust these women because they are like themselves and provide continuity in child rearing, which reinforces their own value system. But to the extent that Born and Raised parents are beginning to see the value of early childhood education as preparation for school success, they may find nonprofessional babysitters lacking and seek more educationally oriented child care arrangements as their children approach school age.

Chapter 4

Two More Babysitters

Two women, among the caregivers I interviewed, differed markedly from the rest—Thelma and Caryl. In talking to Born and Raised babysitters, I had formed a general picture of caregivers, both relatives and neighbors, who on the whole provided reliable services of a quality acceptable to the parents who used them. Most of the Born and Raised babysitters I talked to appeared to me to provide what could be termed adequate care—neither as harmful as bad child care can be, nor, for the most part, as beneficial as good care should be (Keyserling, 1972; Modigliani, 1990).

Of course, I was surveying a rather narrow spectrum of established babysitters within a particular group. In all probability there were cases of worse and better child care. But I think I would have heard of any well-known, long-term Born and Raised babysitters whom parents had found to be harmful to children. And I would also have been told of any providers so outstanding that they might have provided the community with models of excellence.

Thelma and Caryl are not examples of bad care and good care— neither can be so easily categorized—but they do illustrate how babysitter care can differ from the general patterns I found among the established Born and Raised babysitters. Thelma cares for children only in her own family, but her story is different from the care by grandmothers described as "ideal" by Born and Raised parents such as Suzanne. Thelma's account reveals how problematical care by relatives can be when a family is beset by poverty and social disorganization. Caryl's story illustrates another side of babysitting. Unlike the Born and Raised babysitters who have made no move toward the state's new registration system, Caryl is struggling to achieve professional status as a licensed day care provider.

THELMA'S STORY: A FAMILY TRYING TO COPE

Thelma was one of the first babysitters I interviewed. I was looking for Born and Raised women who cared for children, and a community health worker put me in touch with her. Although she was born in a neighboring community and has lived in East Urban all her adult life, Thelma does not count herself as Born and Raised. She identified her maiden name as English and proudly explained that her family had been in America since the seventeenth century. During the interview she repeatedly stressed how she came from a higher-class background than her neighbors, although she claimed to have no racial prejudice against them. She is proud of the fact that her father worked in a bank and that she grew up in what she described as a middle-class neighborhood of two-family houses where the fathers went off to jobs and the mothers stayed home. This had not been the pattern of the previous generation in Thelma's family. Her grandmother, when widowed with nine children, had supported her family by working as a seamstress and with the help of her older children living at home, who contributed part of their earnings to the household. In telling me her history, Thelma described a family that had bettered itself in the previous generation only to fall on hard times in the present one.

Thelma is now divorced with three grown children, Suki, 28, Wayne, 26, and Grace, 24. Her tenement apartment, where the interview took place, has four small rooms and is comfortably furnished. On the day I visited, we sat in the kitchen along with Thelma's mother, whom Thelma cares for every day and who lives in a nearby town. Thelma is in her mid-fifties, thin, quick motioned, and has a look of aging glamour. She wore an attractive sweater and pants, and her shoulder-length hair was held back by a hairband. Her mother, an older and more tired version of Thelma, sat slumped in a kitchen chair, dressed in shapeless clothes and bedroom slippers.

When I asked Thelma about her work as a babysitter, she told me the story of her life, how the tangled family relationships and sporadic employment in her own and her children's lives have determined her child care work. After completing high school Thelma went to business school, where she met her husband. They dreamed of opening an advertising agency together. Instead, her husband "went on drink and drugs" and entered a life of organized crime in East Urban, highjacking trucks at gunpoint. Thelma says she also drank, accompanying her husband to bars to try to keep him from other women. Three children were born in 5 years, and when the youngest, Grace, was still an infant, Thelma's husband deserted her, leaving no trace.

Thelma's mother did not want to be a babysitter for her grand-children because that would have meant coming into East Urban. Instead, the grandmother took an office job to supplement her husband's retirement income so that they could help to support Thelma and her children. When the children were of school age, Thelma found a job as an embroidery designer, and her father took over her household, caring for the three children, doing the laundry, and buying the groceries. "He was the Suzy Homemaker and I was like a child again," is how Thelma described this period. Her father would pick the children up from school and then lock them in their apartment while he went to pick Thelma up from work and to shop for groceries on the way home.

After Thelma's father died, her children began to "get out of hand." Thelma's job required her to leave the house in the morning before the children had to leave for school. Truancy became a habit, and their grades plummeted. They were given their own latchkey and invited friends over after school, children Thelma didn't want in her house. When welfare authorities met with Thelma and accused her of "poor home training," she feared that the state might take the children away from her. Wayne, at 15, drank, took drugs, and was "kicked out" of school. Thelma would call in sick at her job to make court appearances on his behalf. Suki, at 16, became pregnant by Tyrone, a 17-year-old black maintenance worker, but was "allowed" to graduate from high school. Thelma, distressed about her life and her children, had a nervous breakdown but, for reasons she did not explain, was not at that time eligible for public assistance, so that Wayne became head of the household and the family lived on his earnings.

When Thelma first learned that Suki was expecting a child, she considered "stuffing my belly" to appear pregnant so that she could later claim the newborn child and raise it as her own. But Suki wanted to keep her baby, whom she named Margaret, and she and Tyrone were married. Soon afterward the couple were divorced when Tyrone fathered a baby by another woman, whom he subsequently married. A single mother, Suki found a night job working in a bar. At that point Thelma took Margaret in to live with her and assumed full responsibility for her care. Thelma explained, "Margaret is racially mixed, not strictly white, but I believe in taking care of your own. I took Margaret because it was easier on me and on the child." Margaret lived with Thelma for 10 years (Suki had her own apartment) and was considered part of Thelma's household. In addition, Thelma has maintained a "good relationship" with Tyrone and babysits as needed for his three children by his second wife. Tyrone's mother lives nearby, but, according to Thelma, is seldom used for babysitting because she is illiterate and cannot help the children with their homework.

Thelma's son, Wayne, on whose earnings the family depended, was in and out of jail, "a punk," according to Thelma. Thelma blames this on growing up with the "wrong kids." Wayne's gang of boys were known as petty thieves constantly dodging the police. Soon after Wayne assumed financial responsibility for the family, he brought his 16-year-old girl friend, a high school dropout and an alcoholic, to live in the apartment. "I inherited her and her dog," Thelma recalled, still bristling at the thought, "but how could I turn them out?" Finally, the girl left with Wayne, and soon after that they "broke up."

Grace, Thelma's youngest child, married her childhood sweetheart, Hector, a Hispanic. Grace had a church wedding ("she wasn't pregnant"), and she and her husband earned enough at their jobs to make a down payment on a house before their daughter, Joanne, was born. Grace had hoped to be able to give up her job as a cashier and to stay at home with her baby, but shortly after Joanne's birth Hector lost his job. He collected unemployment insurance and stayed at home to care for the baby while Grace went back to work. "But he got tired and would leave the baby with his mother," explained Thelma. "Right away that child belonged to the paternal side. That's the Spanish culture. They belong to the father."

With a second baby on the way, Hector found a job as a salesman. But when the new baby was 2 weeks old, Hector left Grace to live with a woman he had met at his new job. Grace applied for public assistance but was ineligible, so Hector's sister took over the care of the two children. The children, now six and seven, stay with Hector's parents during the week. Grace cares for them on weekends and picks them up after school to help them with their homework at her apartment. On weekdays she takes them to their grandparents for the night.

Suki, Thelma's other daughter, is now married to her second husband, Theo, whom she met when he was boarding with Thelma as an illegal alien from Chile. (He sometimes entered Thelma's apartment from the roof to escape the authorities.) Suki and Theo, whose immigration status is now legal, have a 2-year-old son, Lenny. Thelma regularly cares for Lenny during the day because Suki and Theo both hold jobs. Suki works as a health aide during the day and as a waitress at night.

Thelma agreed to care for Lenny for 10 hours a day for $35 a week, but she feels exploited. She is often called on to babysit for longer than the agreed-upon 10 hours, and she is not paid regularly. Suki and Theo "get behind" in the payments. Thelma says, "I'm an old softie. They ask, 'Can you wait?' And I give in. It gets so mixed up when it's family. It's not like dealing with a neighbor." Thelma waved a book of bills and receipts at me to illustrate her point and protested, "To have to stand there and hand your family receipts!" Ruefully, she added, "And since they chipped in for a color TV for me, I'm ashamed to even ask for their money."

Suki and Theo have had difficulties in their marriage as a result of Suki's working at two jobs. Even though Suki receives $35 a week from her first husband, Tyrone, in child support for her daughter Margaret—money that goes for Catholic school tuition and school uniforms—she finds she must still work at two jobs to support her family. Since Theo did not want full responsibility for child care during Suki's evening work hours, Thelma does more nighttime babysitting. The stress, however, is taking its toll, and Suki, according to Thelma, has begun to act "like an angry monster." Theo, resentful of child care, housework, and Suki's bad moods, moved out and got his own apartment. Since then Thelma hasn't charged anything for Lenny's care. "They got in a jam," she says, "and now I have to get them out." Theo's mother, another grandmother who might also have been enlisted to help care for Lenny, speaks only Spanish, which Lenny doesn't understand.

Thelma no longer cares for Margaret, now 12, who has moved back with Suki. Suki worried about Margaret's safety in Thelma's neighborhood with its drug-infested blocks. But Suki's apartment proved to be equally unsafe, and a man broke in while Margaret was there alone. Now Margaret goes to the home of a classmate after school. Margaret and her classmate, another 12-year-old girl, keep each other company and care for the classmate's 4-year-old brother until his mother returns from work. Margaret, according to Thelma, is "pretty and smart" but says of herself, "I don't belong to anybody."

Thelma's son Wayne has recently moved in with his new girl friend, Louise, and her son from a previous marriage. The boy is cared for by his maternal grandmother when his mother is at her job. Louise is now pregnant, and she and Wayne are planning to be married. Thelma wonders if she will be expected to care for Wayne's new baby in addition to Lenny. Thelma worries about caring for both an infant and a toddler. As it is, she has difficulty caring for both her mother and Lenny. Since she's on the second floor, she has to "bump" the carriage down while Lenny waits on the landing. Because it's so difficult to manage both a load of groceries and a small child, she finds that she shops for smaller amounts and more frequently in "Mom and Pop" stores and spends twice as much. "I can't buy six bags once a week because I can't get to the supermarket. I can't get to the bank. I can't go out until 7:30 at night. I want personal time."

Nevertheless Thelma prefers babysitting for her extended family to working at other employment. At her caseworker's urging, Thelma had recently taken a job at the county welfare office but found that she disliked the "redundant paperwork." By working she lost her food stamps and her medical care, and earned only $5 to $10 more a week than she was receiving from public assistance. She quit and now says she is happier and "worth more to society" as the family babysitter.

CHILD CARE IN A TROUBLED FAMILY

Thelma's story illustrates how child care has been provided in one family over four generations, a family plagued by problems of divorce, poverty, crime, addiction, and, in at least Thelma's case, emotional instability. When Thelma's husband left her with three young children and no financial support, she relied on her father to care for herself and her children. When he died, Thelma found it so difficult to care for her adolescent children on her own that she ran the risk of having them removed from her home by welfare authorities and suffered a nervous breakdown. Nevertheless Thelma's daughter Suki, unable to maintain a stable marriage and finding it difficult to care for her own children, turned to Thelma for child care.

Over the years Thelma has provided a considerable part of the care of not only her grandchildren, but of other children within the family network and her own mother. In addition to the daily care of her mother, she assumed the long-term, full-time care of Suki's daughter Margaret; full-day care of Suki's son Lenny; temporary custodial care of her son Wayne's adolescent girl friend; and occasional care of her ex-son-in-law's children. Now she may also be asked to care for her son Wayne's new baby. Just as Thelma's father stepped in to help her with child care when her husband deserted her, so Thelma has tried to help her daughters during their faltering marriages. As she says of Suki and her present husband, Theo, "They got in a jam, and now I have to get them out." Thelma sees child care as an additional and unsustainable burden on marriages already strained by emotional difficulties and financial insecurity. By assuming the duties of child care herself—even at the price of curtailing her own freedom—she hopes to relieve the pressures on her children's beleaguered families.

Thelma is not the only relative available for babysitting, however. Within the tangled skeins of Thelma's family, the lines of responsibility for child care are not obvious. Nor is this a family with a unified heritage to provide a commonly accepted way to bring up children. Each new child calls for decisions to be made on how child care will be shared within the family as it extends across present and former marriages and relationships and between generations. Who should be included as family—Suki's ex-husband's children by his present wife, or Wayne's girl friend's child by a former husband? Decisions also involve gender—should the women assume the primary responsibility for child care? And they involve economics—in whose homes will children be safe, adequately fed, and well clothed?

Decisions about child care involve race and ethnicity—should the children of black or Hispanic parentage be cared for in black or Hispanic homes? Thelma, for example, recognizes the social stigma of her granddaughter Margaret's color ("not strictly white"), but her belief in "taking care of your own" overrides the issue of race. Grace's children, on the other hand, have been claimed by their Hispanic paternal grandparents, Hector's mother and father. Thelma attributes this to ethnicity, the "Spanish culture" ("they belong to the father"). But in fact, at this point Hector's parents can provide a more stable and financially secure family for the children than either of their parents or Thelma can. Thelma now worries that if Suki and Theo separate permanently, their son Lenny might go to "the father's side" because Theo would want his son in a Hispanic household.

Thelma extends her child care responsibilities for relatives' children to the offspring of her daughter Suki's ex-husband Tyrone's three children. The reason she gave is that Tyrone's mother is illiterate and can't help them with their homework. A similar decision has been made in regard to Grace's children. Their custodial grandparents, because they are Spanish-speaking, do not assume responsibility for the children's after-school homework supervision. In these cases, when children are of an age to move outward from the family and into the public institutions of schooling, the educational qualifications of care-givers may take precedence over other claims.

Who will take care of Wayne and Louise's expected baby is not yet clear to Thelma. Since Louise's mother has already assumed the care of an older child (Louise's son by an earlier marriage), she would seem to be the obvious choice, being the maternal grandmother and available for child care. Louise is steadily employed, however, and Wayne's employment history has been spotty. If Wayne should be expected to provide child care while Louise is at her job, Thelma may be anticipating having to take over Wayne's share. She has already seen her sons-in-law, Hector and Theo, prove to be unwilling to take on child care duties during their wives' working hours.

Of all the third-generation fathers, only Tyrone, Suki's first husband, provides regular child support—$35 a week, for Margaret. Although Margaret's care has been shared by her mother and grandmother, the child support money is kept separate from general household money by earmarking it for Margaret's parochial school tuition and uniforms, thus making it clear that the money goes directly and completely to Margaret, not to the general household expenses of her custodians. Margaret, now 12, has assumed responsibility for her own after-school care and even helps to provide care for a younger child. As she herself realizes, she no longer "belongs" to anybody.

In addition to grandchildren, Thelma cares for her mother, thus repaying the previous generation for care provided for her and her children. In Thelma's parents' case, it was her father who provided the child care for his grandchildren and her mother who took a job to help support them. Whether Thelma's children will in turn feel obligated to provide care for her because she cared for them and their children is a question for the future. Thelma has preferred babysitting to outside employment. Her children may have different priorities.

In Thelma's family, child care is apportioned out among relatives, but this solution is far from "ideal." Because the family as a whole is characterized by economic stress, child care takes place within a framework of low-paying jobs, illegal employment, unemployment, shifting family relationships, petty crime, alcoholism, and marital discord. Unlike Born and Raised families who share a common background, Thelma's family crosses class, ethnic, and racial barriers, which adds further difficulties to making child care arrangements. Different members of the family draw on different cultural heritages with differing ideas of what is best for their children.

Thelma's caseworker has urged her to take a job outside her home. Her mother also urges Thelma to give up babysitting, telling her that she should not keep trying "to pick up the pieces" of her children's lives. But despite this advice, Thelma persists in "looking after her own." Although Thelma's family would appear in need of professional, reliable child care, no family members have yet sought child care beyond what is available from their relatives.

CARYL'S STORY: STRUGGLING TOWARD A DREAM

Caryl's story is a very different one from Thelma's. Caryl is the only babysitter I found in East Urban who has not only been professionally trained but is also planning to apply for a day care license. I learned about Caryl from Yolanda, a former Head Start teacher. I had been asking Yolanda if she knew any babysitters who took care of groups of children, as opposed to only one or two. Yolanda could think of only one—her friend Caryl, whom she had met as a fellow worker in Head Start. When I telephoned Caryl, she readily agreed to be interviewed.

Caryl and her husband, who are black, own their house, which is in one of the "nicer" parts of town, but the buildings on their block vary from well kept to rundown. From the outside, Caryl's building does not look so bad. It is four stories high, with a front door opening onto the top of the stoop. But as soon as I opened the front door and saw the scruffy entryway I knew I was not in the sort of "clean" house that many mothers expect from babysitters. A door at the end of the front hallway leads into a good-sized kitchen with windows overlooking a cluttered backyard. When I arrived, Caryl was in the midst of creating a handmade "sink" for children's play by inserting a metal foil baking pan into a plastic-covered cardboard frame. Although the building is in bad repair and infested with roaches that constantly scuttle along the kitchen walls, the place looked cozy and comfortable. In the center of the kitchen is a table where the interview took place, with Caryl readily agreeing to be tape recorded.

As we talked, a toddler in the adjoining room played contentedly with toys. This room, next to the kitchen, used to be the family's "den," but Caryl has converted it into a place for her day care children to play. A large fish tank and caged hamster have displaced the family television set. Toys and picture books fill the former bookshelves, and Caryl also set up a doll corner and a play "office" where children can use an electric adding machine and other office supplies. She mentioned modeling clay, crayons, and puzzles as examples of other materials she has on hand.

Caryl babysits in her home for a total of eight children, most of them after school and on staggered schedules that keep her within the legal limit of no more than five children at a time. But unlike the other babysitters I interviewed, Caryl plans to apply for a day care license and to earn a B.A. in early childhood education. She began to work professionally with children when she was hired to work at the East Urban Head Start program. While there she earned her Child Development Associate credential through an inservice training program and in the process accumulated 30 college credits. More recently she commuted to the City to work as an aide in a demonstration child care center attached to a prestigious college of education.

When she finally decided to do family day care on her own and to complete her degree, she took a year's leave from her job as aide. She now does babysitting during the day and attends college courses at night and on weekends. This has meant giving up her $14,000-a-year salary, and benefits, for babysitting work that brings less than $75 a week. Providentially, her family is covered by benefits from her husband's job as a unionized warehouse worker. But even with her oldest daughter, who lives at home, contributing to the mortgage payments, Caryl says this is a "hard year" for the family financially.

Caryl, who feels she has "a special way with children," has cared for many, as a mother, a volunteer, and a professional caregiver. She and her husband had two children of their own and then adopted five foster children. At one time, before she became a paid babysitter, Caryl not only took care of her own children and additional foster children but opened her house to neighborhood children as well. Now, in addition to providing family day care, she has six children and two grandchildren living at home. She also, as a volunteer, coordinates a tutoring program, leads a Girl Scout troop, and teaches Sunday School.

In the absence of state family day care or group home licensing, Caryl must apply for licensing as a day care center if she wants to legally care for more than five children at a time. Accordingly, she has applied for a home improvement loan to remodel her house so that it can be licensed as a center. "I feel there are going to be people out there who are going to be needing this service," she said, "and if it's something I'd like to do, why not do it?" Caryl's mother, who lives two blocks away, has volunteered to work in the center as Caryl's assistant.

Caryl explained her reasons for completing her degree and seeking a license this way:

> I plan on having a day care, but I want the parents to know
> that I'm qualified because I don't believe in just babysitting. I
> don't believe that you should just sit there and babysit. Between
> the ages that I work with, which is between two and five, there
> are so many growths going on in the children that I think they
> need more than just a babysitter. I want parents to know that
> I'm qualified to deal with their children. I know what to expect
> at certain areas in their lives. A lot of people want a piece of
> paper [a license]. That's why I decided to go back to school.
> Because I know that I'm qualified to do certain things and so
> do the people in close contact with me. But then you come

across people who would prefer a piece of paper. So you give them a piece of paper.

Caryl plans to care for "preschoolers in a full-day setting" because she anticipates that federal welfare reform legislation will lead to mothers' putting their children in child care at earlier ages. She has made professional affiliations by registering with the county child care coordinating council and with the local welfare-to-work program, which has sent her one parent. "I don't mind the paperwork," she says. She also plans to apply for insurance and for participation in the federal child care food program.

Since the parents of the children she now cares for are low-income, Caryl charges everyone the same fee of $1 an hour, which includes food. She thinks "maybe" she will raise her rates to $1.50 when she is licensed because at her present low rates she is under constant pressure to take more children. "Everybody tells me I should raise my rates," she admitted, but she is generous-hearted and reluctant to charge more to her low-income, largely minority parents. "It's not easy for parents to go out and have to work," she said, remembering her own past, "then have a big child care bill. I know when I was doing it, it was hard."

Caryl believes that the child care she gives in her home is probably better than center-based care. "I don't know the quality," she says of East Urban's day care centers. "I just feel that if too many children are in a center and they don't have enough help—if the help is kind of burned out or underpaid, which they really are—the parents are not going to get the service they expect. And of course the little ones aren't going to say, 'Someone didn't feel good today, so I wasn't cared for that well.'"

When Caryl's own children were preschool age, she had her mother to help and would not have considered using a center.

> I personally feel that no one can take care of them as well as family—which is wrong, because what if someone thinks that of me? Now times have changed to where there are a lot more parents going out to work, where there is no family around. Babysitting is the closest to doing it yourself. It's only one step away.

Although Caryl's oldest daughter has said she would like to join her mother once she is licensed, Caryl has reservations about including her. She told her, "You're young. You haven't done much in the world yet. This isn't going to give you much money, and you're not going to get much out of it except pleasure. If you plan on doing a lot of things in your life, you're going to have to look elsewhere." Caryl has no doubts, however, about her own calling as a day care provider. "I'm at an age where I've done whatever I wanted to," she said, "and I know this is what I want to do. I know this is where my heart is. I don't have to go looking to see if this is where my dream is because I know it is."

When I praised Caryl for what seemed to me an extraordinary dedication to helping children, she answered:

> It's because I like doing it. It's like adopting the kids. My husband had to put a stop to it because he told me I couldn't have all the children in the world. I could only have but so many. I don't see this as being anything extraordinary or fantastic. As a matter of fact, at times I see it as being kind of selfish because it's something I really enjoy doing. Like I said, he said I couldn't have all the children. This is another way of doing it. I'll have someone else's now.

DECIDING TO BECOME LICENSED

Among the East Urban babysitters I interviewed, Caryl was unique both in taking college courses in early childhood education and in planning to apply for a license for child care. She is devoted to nurturing children but, unlike the other babysitters I interviewed, she views her work as a career and uses professional terms to describe it. She sometimes refers to her work as "babysitting," but also calls it by its more professional term, "family day care." She describes her future plan as taking care of "preschoolers in a full-day setting," again using the professional terminology. When she describes her qualifications she speaks of being able to respond appropriately to developmental "growths" or stages—a standard used by professional early childhood educators.

After bringing up her own large family and foster children as well, Caryl first encountered professionally trained teachers of young children when she worked for Head Start. There she was exposed to a model of early childhood education and child care. Since the Head Start program encourages its staff to participate in inservice training programs, Caryl was able to earn the Child Development Associate credential during her stay. She has since had experience in a high quality model day care center at the laboratory school where she worked as an aide. As a result of her job experience and professional training, her family day care program bears a professional stamp that sets it apart from babysitters whose only model for day care is the experience of caring for their own children.

Despite its scruffy appearance, Caryl's room for children's play had more of the materials and equipment associated with high quality professional care than the other babysitters' homes I visited. The doll corner and the children's "office" encourage dramatic play—a form of activity that professional educators consider essential for young children's learning but that was never mentioned by other babysitters. Caryl had also introduced animals—fish and a hamster—for children to care for, another activity favored by early childhood educators. Other babysitters I visited, perhaps fearing possible injury, kept children away from family pets. (One babysitter's caged parrot, for example, was kept in a room where children were not allowed.)

Caryl provided children with modeling clay, crayons, and puzzles, which, probably because they are commercialized and advertised widely, were also used by the other babysitters in East Urban. But unlike other babysitters, she also made toys by hand to suit the children's interests. The "sink" she was constructing when I arrived was to be added to the doll corner as an additional prop for dramatic play. Although creating materials suitable for children's particular stages of growth and interests is a mark of professional early childhood educational programs, no other babysitters I observed made their own toys or encouraged dramatic play.

When Caryl thought about her choice of work, she considered her personal aptitude for the job—she "likes" doing it—but she also thought analytically about how changes in East Urban family life would create a demand for her services. Like other babysitters, she recognized that more mothers were "going out" to work, but she had also thought about specific legislation that would influence mothers' employment. She knew that federal welfare reform would create a demand for family day care, and she had already applied to the local work incentive program for referrals.

Not only did Caryl recognize the value of professional college courses in early childhood education for her work in day care, but she sought help from other professional organizations concerned with child care. She had been in touch with the local child care coordinating council and planned to apply for the federal child care food program.

Caryl showed none of the Born and Raised reticence to work with social service agencies; instead she used them as a source of support for her work.

Several factors might account for the marked difference in Caryl's outlook. For one, Caryl and her husband had a long and fulfilling experience in providing foster care, a program administered through the Department of Social Services. No doubt they had also had governmental help in financing the buying of their house. Caryl is used to the paperwork required for dealing with agencies and finds it no major obstacle. Although she is able to draw help with child care from her own family—both her mother and daughter have offered their services—she also knows how to find technical services from bureaucratic sources outside the family.

Although she plans to apply for a license, Caryl skeptically refers to it as a "piece of paper." She is confident of her qualifications because of her training. "I know that I'm qualified," she says, but she also recognizes that "a lot of people want a piece of paper." Since Caryl plans to take referrals from state agencies, she is realistic in recognizing the need for official status. Caryl has a strong sense of community service and is committed to serving low-income minority parents. If she is to earn a decent income, however, she cannot depend on the low fees she now charges. She will need to be subsidized by the state in order to keep fees affordable to her parents.

The parents who now have children in Caryl's care must have decided that the good qualities of her program outweigh the limitations of the surroundings—the roach infestation and the general shabbiness of the building. In its present condition the premises would never pass inspection for licensing. But if Caryl can manage the home improvement loan she says she is applying for, the building can be renovated.

Caryl is able to view her professionalism as no threat to her status as nurturer. She lapses easily from her professional vocabulary to refer to "the little ones" in day care, and sees her work as a career but also as an extension of family. She has nurtured widening circles of children, first her own, then foster children whom she made her own, and now children in care. But this generosity of spirit is also a danger to economic survival. Caryl sees her work as a public service, similar to her tutoring, her Scout work, and her Sunday school teaching, and she charges less than her services are worth at market rates. The day I visited, one of the after-school children who also comes at lunchtime brought along two friends for company. Caryl didn't mind. The child's fees were paid by her grandmother, who looked after her full-time while holding a job herself. Caryl would not think of charging her more. Caryl's feelings of service to others are what animate her work. But in order to succeed as a professional she will have to balance her idealism with the economic realities of day care.

IN THE ABSENCE OF A SYSTEM

Neither Thelma nor Caryl would call herself a Born and Raised East Urbanite, although both were born and grew up in the area. Thelma identifies herself as "American" and from a middle-class family fallen on hard times of unemployment and family dissolution. Caryl's identity comes from being black and a member of a family that has pulled itself from poverty into a stable position of steady employment, home ownership in a good neighborhood, and college education. In some ways these two families are on opposite paths—Thelma's moving downward in a socioeconomic sense and Caryl's moving upward. Neither family falls within the patterns of child care that I found within the Born and Raised community—patterns that have been maintained by solidly established working-class families who share assumptions about child care based on ethnic identity. Born and Raised parents describe child care by relatives as ideal, but in Thelma's family, care by relatives is beset by problems that threaten the well-being of the children. Born and Raised babysitters see no need for professional training or for becoming licensed, but Caryl recognizes the value to her program of early childhood education and of becoming licensed.

At this point neither Thelma nor Caryl has what she wants and needs, and the present state of East Urban child care services works against them both. Thelma's family would benefit from reliable, professional child care, but East Urban has no licensed family day care program offering such care. For Thelma's family there is no choice but to make the best of their limited family resources.

Caryl would seem to have the makings of a high quality, professionally trained caregiver, but she appears to be battling against the odds to achieve professional status. Studying for her degree has meant financial sacrifice—giving up her regular job to babysit for the minimal fees her low-income parents are able to pay. Further financing will be necessary to improve her home to meet licensing standards. With state funding, Caryl's path would be eased, but it would also help if she could establish herself as a licensed family day care provider as a first step toward becoming a day care center.

The stories of Thelma and Caryl illustrate families who lack (in Thelma's case) or aspire to more than (in Caryl's case) the largely adequate child care provided by the arrangements described as "ideal" by Born and Raised families. In the absence of a state-regulated family day care system, East Urban children may not be protected from the worst of care, and they may not have access to the best.

Chapter 5

Views of Child Care
in Times Past

Born and Raised parents gave me the impression that using day care centers invited disapproval. Centers were for "others." "We take care of our own," they told me. I wanted to know more about why day care centers were so disparaged when child care was so needed. Such strong opinions, I assumed, must be deeply embedded in past experiences and community values. What was the history of day care in East Urban, I wondered, and how had centers come by their present reputation among Born and Raised parents? Unfortunately, East Urban had no expert on the local history of child welfare. Instead, I groped for clues amid the reminiscences I was hearing about "the way things used to be."

THE COMMUNITY DAY NURSERY

One name cropped up repeatedly as people talked of the past. It was the Community Day Nursery, which, I eventually learned, was a nursery "ministering to the needs of children of poor working mothers" that had preceded all other day care centers and had lasted almost a century until it closed in the 1970s. Depending on whom I talked to, I was given different views of the Day Nursery.

Michelle, the young mother I had interviewed who told me about her alcoholic father and her mother who took a job to support their family of eight children, had a vivid first-hand memory of the Day Nursery. Her younger brother had been cared for there while their mother was at work, and Michelle had the job of picking him up each afternoon after school. She felt sorry for her brother having to stay at the nursery and thought he was treated meanly. Some days she would find that he had been shut up alone in the boiler room as a punishment.

I could imagine the dismay of a parent on hearing of such treatment, and I asked Michelle how her mother had reacted. Recalling her mother's life, Michelle gave a realistic answer.

Well, she was in a very desperate situation. My father was an alcoholic. He was abusive. She got him out of the house and she went back to work. She had been home in a bad situation for a bunch of years, so I think for her it was liberating and a relief. But she didn't like it, and she does have a lot of guilt associated with it. But you either sink or swim, and she chose to swim.

I got a more detached opinion from an educator who had moved to East Urban in the 1960s and had been so appalled by the poor schools that she started one of her own. When she first arrived in East Urban she found that the Day Nursery provided the only day care in town. She described it rather disparagingly as a place run "with a sense of mission" by "volunteer housewives" for Italian mothers who, for one reason or another, were forced to take jobs and to seek care for their children during the working day. In the educator's view, the Day Nursery lacked professional standards but provided adequate custodial care. She summed it up as a "you-could-eat-off-the-floor kind of environment, not stimulating but clean." I began to form a picture of a grim and heartless institution where mothers would leave their children only as a last resort.

THE BABY CONGRESS

Still on the track of the history of child care in East Urban, I went to the local public library, an imposing Victorian brick building donated to the city by an early manufacturer. I found nothing in the card catalogue about child care, but a helpful librarian directed me to a bookcase with locked glass doors, devoted to local history. Looking through the shelves of musty and tattered volumes, I came across a scrapbook labeled "The Baby Congress." Inside were pasted newspaper accounts of a competition held in 1918 to find the healthiest infant in East Urban. Someone, perhaps one of the organizers of the contest, had kept every newspaper account of the competition, and the fact that these filled an entire scrapbook attested to the event's importance. Reading these yellowed clippings gave me some idea of how the prosperous middle class viewed the child care of the poor at the time of World War I.

The contest was held as part of the city's war effort and as a response to President Wilson's declaration that the high national infant mortality rate was posing a threat to America's future security. East Urban determined to do its part by helping to improve the survival chances of infants born to poor immigrant families. "Welfare stations" were established for treating infants' health needs, especially malnutrition, and because health officials judged the diet of immigrant families to be unhealthy, mothers were instructed in the newest dietary theories. These lessons in nutrition, designed to correct the "abuses" of ethnic cooking, were apparently not received with enthusiasm, because welfare officials complained of "parent apathy." The authorities also learned something about what were to be persisting problems of child care, for they reported that some mothers "make eight dollars caring for other people's children and neglect their own."

Finally I gave up trying to find any account of the Community Day Nursery, but by this time the librarian had become interested in what I was looking for. When she saw that I had exhausted my search through the books, she locked up the case and offered some information of her own. She said that she remembered how, as a child, she used to pass by a day nursery in her neighborhood. She had been told that it was a place for children whose fathers left them there because their mothers had died. That had seemed a terrible fate for a child, and the librarian had always felt sad when she saw the day nursery children.

The librarian herself had grown up in a family where both parents worked, but she never identified herself with the day nursery children. Born of Italian immigrant parents, she, "like all Italian and Irish in those days," was cared for by relatives while her father worked as a trainman and her mother as a seamstress (because her father was subject to layoffs, particularly during the Depression). When the librarian became a mother herself, she stayed at home with her three sons until the youngest was 10. Then she started to work at the library. This pattern is being repeated in the next generation, for her daughters-in-law plan to wait until their children are of school age before taking outside employment.

With her family history of relative care and her own childhood memories of day care children as deprived and pitiable, I was fairly certain that the librarian would not consider a day care center for her own family's children. But I wanted to hear her opinion of centers in her own words. What did she know about East Urban's present day care, I asked. "It's for the welfare mothers to get them to work" was her prompt and emphatic answer.

ROSE'S HISTORY

I continued to ask people about the Community Day Nursery and finally learned the name of someone who would surely tell me more about this early day care effort. Rose, I heard, not only was a past president of the nursery but was also in charge of its archives. When I interviewed her, she was able to fill in for me the story of the Day Nursery, but she also told me the story of her own family, which provided a Born and Raised counterpoint to her account of her charitable activities.

Rose's apartment was on a block where I had previously interviewed a "yuppie" mother who had proudly showed off the elaborate restored woodwork in her apartment, which, she explained, showed that the building had originally been built as a home for a single prosperous family. Rose also took pride in her home. She explained that the block had historically been one where "better people" lived. When Rose and her husband moved in, they were the first Italians there. Most of their neighbors were German, and the German social club (now condominiums) was a few doors down. Rose and her husband bought their building from a single woman who had grown up there with her parents. Coming from the Italian part of town, Rose was amazed that such a small family—only three people—were the sole occupants of a four-story house. Rose and her husband immediately converted the building into apartments and moved with their three children into the bottom two floors. To enter, I found I had to go down and under the front steps and through a dark little passage at ground level that led directly into Rose's apartment.

Our interview took place in the dining room, which was formally furnished and was lighted, though the ceiling was very low, by a chandelier. An oval table covered with a lace tablecloth was set with an elaborate glass centerpiece flanked by glass candlesticks with glass "candles." A corner cupboard was jammed with china. On the sideboard two framed photographs of Rose's grandchildren occupied the place of honor, and other family photographs and civic awards lined the walls. Through an open doorway I could see the kitchen, which looked out on the back garden and was a much more light and cheerful place than the dining room.

I was surprised when Rose told me she was 71. Small and slim, dressed in a powder blue pants suit with a fresh-from-the-hairdresser blond hairdo, she had a youthful, quick, energetic manner that belied her age. The fact that we were to talk in the dining room rather than at the kitchen table showed how formal Rose expected this interview to be, and she had prepared for it by spreading out across the table a series of manila folders containing the records of the Community Day Nursery.

According to these accounts, the Nursery was founded in 1885 to aid working mothers and their children. A brochure published in 1974 explained, "The Nursery's object and purpose was to provide a suitable haven in which 'day care' could be given to children who came from homes where it was mandatory for the mother to work." Rose emphasized that the Nursery was only for mothers who were married. Another East Urban charitable institution, the Smithfield Home, was described in the brochure as being for children of "widowed parents." (This, not the Community Nursery, was evidently the place that the librarian had remembered passing as a child.)

A newspaper picture of the Community Day Nursery's board showed its women members, all in hats, at a tea party presided over by their president, who poured tea from a silver pot. Rose explained that the nursery's boards had always been "German ladies" and were usually the same women who served on the East Urban Women's Club board. Rose was proud to have been asked to join the board and particularly to have been made president the following year.

It was under Rose's leadership as president that the Nursery decided to close. She explained its demise as due primarily to lack of funds. The original funding for the nursery had come from legacies. When these became insufficient, the board was unwilling either to raise more funds (because the ladies were "too elderly") or to accept government grants (because "they didn't want the government to tell them what to do"). Another reason for the decline of the Day Nursery was a shrinking enrollment—due in part, she said, to the fact that the Catholic schools had started programs for 4-year-olds.

Even though the Community Day Nursery was meant for mothers whose work was "mandatory," these families included no Hispanics, even during the years of the greatest Hispanic population growth. Rose explained this by saying that "the fees were too high for Puerto Rican families" (although she had earlier said the fees were very low and that she could remember when they had gone up from 10 cents to 25 cents when she was a child). She further explained the absence of "the Spanish" by saying that "they like to stay within their own." Rose said that the Nursery had been located in what was once an all-Italian neighborhood that gradually "deteriorated" when it became "all Puerto Rican." Hispanic children, she claimed, once set fire to the building. Rose deplored the changes in old, ethnic neighborhoods. She remembered that when she first heard that "Spics" were coming to

East Urban, she asked who they were. People explained that they were Puerto Ricans and described people who "hang out of windows and don't put up curtains." "Give them 10 years and they'll change," Rose answered at the time. "But they haven't," she says now. "They are not like European immigrants. We have to rebuild what they wreck."

When I asked about the program at the Day Nursery, Rose seemed at a loss for an answer, although she said that board members did sometimes help out. The one thing she positively remembered was that the nursery passed state inspection every 3 years. Most of the typed reports in the manila folders pertained to board matters, dispersal of the property, and legalities. None of the records described the children or their activities.

Rose stressed to me that the Day Nursery was a private, not a public, enterprise. She pointed out that it never referred to its services as "day care." "In those days," she said, "there wasn't any 'preschool' or 'day care.' There was just the 'Nursery.'" When I asked Rose what she knew about East Urban day care today, she replied that she had never heard of any "public day care," but after thinking a minute she remembered that she'd heard that some programs had been started in Spanish churches. She is acquainted with the private centers, which she referred to as "preschools" rather than as "day cares." "There are so many springing up," she exclaimed, "and one place even takes babies!"

Although it seems unlikely that Rose would have agreed to be interviewed except on the subject of the Community Day Nursery, she began to talk about her own family as we continued the interview. She described herself as coming from a "poor working family" and said she had emigrated to East Urban from Italy as an infant of 5 months. Her father had arrived first and, once established as an ironworker in East Urban, sent for his wife and two daughters. Rose said that when she was a child, families came over from Italy together, several generations at once, and lived near each other on the same block. Now, she said, Italian immigrants don't come as whole families; they leave their parents behind in Italy.

When Rose was only 2 years old, her mother died in the influenza epidemic, and her father returned to Italy, leaving the little girl to be raised by a childless aunt and uncle, whom Rose soon came to regard as her parents. The aunt had a job in a factory as a hand finisher of coats, but during her working hours she was able to leave Rose with relatives living on the block. Rose explained that in those days children could be cared for by relatives and also by godparents—*comares* and *compares*—who acted as extended family. Another source of child care, she says, was within the building. Since families lived in close quarters, two families to a floor with a shared toilet, they became intimate friends and could be relied on as a child care network.

In the summertime Rose was sent to those of her relatives who rented places near the shore. It was evidently very important to these immigrant families to get their children away from East Urban's hot tenements and factory grime, and to a place near the ocean or a lake, during summer vacation. This still holds true for their descendants. Rose took her own children in the summer to relatives who lived near a lake, and she and her husband were eventually able to buy a second house of their own near the water. They recently sold this house, but only because two of their children married into "shore" families— families who live in East Urban but also own summer houses near the ocean, where grandchildren are welcome.

As a young married woman with three children of her own, Rose lived with her husband above his Italian grocery store (which is now a Spanish bodega), along with her aunt and uncle "parents." Although Rose had worked in a factory between her graduation from high school and her marriage, she had no desire to continue working when her three children were young. The only exception was during the war, when clerks were hard to find. During that time she would sometimes go downstairs and help out in the store, and her aunt watched the children while she was gone.

Two of Rose's children are now married and have moved into homes of their own. Both her married daughter and her daughter-in-law worked as teachers until their children were born, but then gave up their jobs to stay at home. "I'm so happy my daughter opted to stay home," Rose says. "It's sad when mothers have to work. Parents should be with their children when they're growing up unless there's no alternative—when there's a broken home from a divorce." Rose says proudly that she "never had to work" and that "my friends never had to work," but she is not against women taking jobs once their children are older. When she was 47, Rose returned to college and started a satisfying career as a teacher in a nearby Catholic school.

Rose has now retired from her teaching position and once again devotes her time entirely to her family. When her grown son became seriously ill, she moved into his house to help take care of him. She brought her terminally ill aunt home to live with her and conscientiously nursed her to the end because the aunt refused to be cared for in a hospital. And she babysits as often as she can for her two young grandsons.

Rose ended our interview when her husband came home and she had to fix lunch for him. She seemed surprised that the time had gone so fast and even more surprised that she had talked so extensively to a total stranger.

CHILD CARE AND WELFARE

These glimpses into the history of child care in East Urban provided background that helped me to understand some of the present-day attitudes of parents, particularly the Born and Raised, toward publicly supported child care. The Community Day Nursery and the Smithfield Home, East Urban's first "day cares," were established by an altruistic middle class as charitable institutions. The founders' mission was to care for the children of families where the mother had died or where it became "mandatory" for the mother to seek employment. These early nurseries were meant only for the children of the "deserving poor"—parents who had the respectability of marriage and the will to be self-supporting.

Cahan (1989) describes how, during the nineteenth and early twentieth centuries, "two tiers" of early childhood programs evolved in the United States.

> One tier, rooted in the social welfare system, was driven by a desire to reduce welfare payments—with scant attention to the needs of the child. This system of custodial "group child care" for low-income families was in sharp contrast to the second tier—child care rooted in the education system that provided "preschool education," mainly for children of the middle and upper—middle classes. (p. v)

The early welfare efforts in East Urban on behalf of children were established by native-born "Americans" for the benefit of the immigrant poor. By World War I, the earlier German immigrants had been replaced as newcomers by the Irish, and it was largely to this group that the campaign to reduce infant mortality was directed in 1918. Parent education was intended to replace "Old World" child care practices with those based on modern professional standards of care in feeding and hygiene. It is not surprising that the immigrant families, struggling with assimilation and poverty, showed "apathy" toward their reformers.

Within the lifetime of those I interviewed about East Urban's history of institutionalized child care, the Community Day Nursery had first served a largely Italian immigrant population, who evidently had used the service only as a last resort, when families, like Michelle's, had come apart and the father was unable to fulfill his traditional role of provider. If a family put its children in the nursery it was because the regular pattern of care by the mother had become inoperable—the father was an alcoholic, abused his wife, or had deserted the family, or the mother had "deserted" her children through death. As Grubb and Lazerson (1982) found on tracing the history of American welfare policy and its connection to national attitudes toward children, American charitable works result from a combination of humanitarian zeal and condemnation of the poor. Providing public services to children without the demonstration of parental failure would contradict the national presumption of private responsibility for children. Using the Day Nursery was an admission that the usual pattern of maintaining self-sufficiency through family networks had broken down and that parents had been forced to turn to charity at the hands of outsiders—strangers who might punish harshly by locking a child in a boiler room or prize cleanliness at the expense of children's comfort.

The story of the Community Day Nursery also shows how East Urban welfare was implemented during successive waves of immigration. As an earlier wave of German immigrants assumed social status in the city, they became the benefactors of charitable institutions where they had once been the beneficiaries. The board of "German ladies" administered the Day Nursery not only for the benefit of poor Italian newcomers but also, as a way of establishing their own community standing—social climbing through charitable works. When Rose became the first Italian to join the board, she exemplified the social ascendancy of a previous wave of immigrants. She and her husband had "crossed the tracks" from the Italian into the more affluent German part of town to join the company of earlier-entrenched and socially superior families. Being asked to join the Community Day Nursery board was a sign of acceptance.

It is probably more than coincidental, however, that Rose became president of the board during the final years of the Nursery, when it must have been obvious that it was in an untenable financial condition. Rose's main job as board president would not be to pour tea while posing for society page photographers, but to supervise the painful business of selling the nursery property and settling it's accounts. By the time that Rose, an Italian, became head of the board, the new immigrant population was Hispanic. The Nursery's surrounding neighborhood had changed from Italian to Hispanic, but instead of serving the Hispanic families the Nursery closed its doors.

Rose blamed the Nursery's fall in enrollment in part on the availability of Catholic school preschool programs, but since these programs last only half a day and take only 4-year-olds, it does not seem likely that preschool programs could take the place of the full-day care provided at the Nursery for working parents. Rose explained the financial crisis as a shrinking of funds from legacies left by earlier generations to the point where expenses could not be met, yet the women on the Nursery board did not mount a fund-raising drive, nor did they seek public funding. It seems likely that the "German ladies" faced changes in East Urban with which they were unwilling or unable to cope. Private charities had been replaced by programs of public welfare, and the newest immigrant poor, the Hispanics, had not conformed to the pattern established by previous waves of German, Irish, and Italian immigrants, who had followed each other up the ladder of social acceptability.

Rose knew practically nothing about East Urban's present-day public child care services that have replaced those of the Day Nursery. Her impression was that some programs had been formed in "Spanish churches," which fulfilled her expectation that "the Spanish like to stay within their own." The librarian had the impression that public-supported child care was for "welfare mothers." Private charity might once have served a succession of European immigrant populations when they fell on hard times, but today's government welfare programs, in the eyes of these Born and Raised women, are for "another kind" of family, likely to be minority, unmarried, and jobless.

ATTITUDES TOWARD WOMEN'S WORK

Talking first to the librarian and later to Rose, I gathered more evidence of why it is a matter of pride for Born and Raised women to stay at home with their preschool children. These daughters and granddaughters of immigrants have equated mothers' employment with family failure. Arriving at the bottom of East Urban's social ladder and striving always to get ahead, immigrant families have struggled toward a better life, a life made safe from the hardships associated with families who have had to use day care in the past. Their mothers or grandmothers, the first-generation immigrants, often worked in factories or in other low-level and onerous jobs because they had to. If, in the succeeding generations, husbands could find jobs that paid well enough for their wives to be able to stay at home with their young children, this was considered a step up in the world, to a better life than that of their parents, when both husband and wife had to work to support the family. The "ideal" and "traditional" family, described by Born and Raised parents, appears in East Urban to have been more a middle-class than a working-class heritage.

The extent to which the role of women as mothers who care for their children at home is a "traditional" one is a complicated issue. The full-time mother as an ideal may have emerged with the middle class—as Ryan (1981), in a case history of Utica, N.Y., between 1907 and 1865, argues. She analyzed the emergence of a nineteenth-century ideology of middle-class domesticity, with women assuming the role of loving guardians of their children. Pehaps this middle-class attitude was adopted by less well-to-do mothers as well. Degler (1980) estimated that although by the end of the nineteenth century close to 50% of young white women were employed before marriage, few white (as opposed to black) married women worked outside the home. This undoubtedly varied in different communities with different employment opportunities for women. In East Urban, immigrant mothers of young children may have been employed at an unusually high rate because small factories employing women were scattered in neighborhoods with low-cost housing, enabling mothers to work close to home.

Rose, typically, identified herself with stay-at-home mothers, rather than with her aunt who worked as a seamstress, and made it clear that "her sort" (and of course the board members) would never have had to use day care because they would not have been "forced" to take a job when their children were small. It may be that the next generation of women, better educated and with possibilities for interesting careers, will follow a newer middle-class model and choose to work outside the home, even if family finances allow them the option of staying at home. Both of Rose's daughters had professional jobs as teachers before their children were born. These mothers now intend to be at home with their young children but may, as Rose did, take jobs when their children are older. Born and Raised daughters, however, are still expected to care for their aging parents at home as well as for their children. Rose nursed her mother full-time when she was dying, which she would not have been able to do if she had still been teaching.

Women's choosing to work at nurturing their families instead of pursuing careers is now one of the distinctions, in the opinion of Born and Raised East Urbanites, between themselves and the yuppies. Those Born and Raised families who have climbed to the middle class may find, however, that their daughters will choose to take the yuppie path. If younger Born and Raised mothers choose employment over staying at home as a means of self-fulfillment as well as a way to increase family earnings, day care may lose its stigma as a sign of family failure and be viewed instead as a service to families that is both desirable and deserved.

Chapter 6

A Look at Licensed
Day Care Centers

Though my study was designed to learn more about nonregulated child care, it became increasingly obvious to me as I continued my interviews that nonregulated child care and regulated or licensed care were not two totally separate spheres. Families sometimes used both, most commonly using home-based care for their infants and toddlers and then moving to a center as their children reached preschool age. Other reasons for families moving between nonregulated and licensed care had to do with availability, location, cost, convenience, hours of operation, and the center's reputation. It would not make sense to study nonregulated care without looking at its alternative—East Urban's licensed child care.

East Urban has three publicly supported day care centers, where parents pay according to a sliding fee that is government-subsidized, and two private centers, which are operated on a for-profit basis and are for full-paying parents only. In general, the families who use public and private programs are divided by income. To be eligible for subsidized day care, a family of two (about three-quarters of the enrollment of publicly funded centers is from single-parent households) must earn no more than $19,827 a year, but many parents in publicly funded centers earn much less or are on public assistance. Private centers, where fees must cover the full cost of care, are affordable only by families with much higher incomes.

Each of the three publicly supported day care centers has a distinct identity. I was repeatedly told that when Born and Raised parents did decide, for whatever reason, to use a center, they sent their children to Johnson School Day Care, which, of the three centers, had the "best" location—in an old, established, white neighborhood only recently "invaded" by Indians. The La Casa center, I was told, is for Hispanics, and the Elm Street center, located in a rundown neighborhood near the public housing projects, is by reputation where teenage mothers on welfare send their children. When I visited these centers to interview their directors and when I talked to the social services administrator of the programs, I began to better understand the differences between centers, which parents are likely to choose which centers, and how center directors view the parents in their programs. I also learned more about why most Born and Raised, and many other like-minded families in the same economic stratum, are unlikely to use center-based care.

My visits to East Urban's day care centers were brief, and I did not make systematic observations of the programs. My intent was to interview the directors to see how they perceived their centers as part of the overall provision of child care in East Urban. I asked about enrollments, fees, the history of each center, ethnic and racial makeup of the families using the center, and what the directors thought of these families as parents. I had already learned a great deal about what parents thought about centers. By visiting the programs I hoped to learn something of the other side of the picture—how center directors viewed the families that used their services.

I felt on much more familiar ground visiting licensed centers than I had when I visited babysitters. For several years previously, I had been engaged in research and advocacy on child care issues and had visited many day care centers in connection with my work. I had also been professionally trained in early childhood education at the Bank Street College of Education and was familiar with the professional terms in which center directors usually described their work. As in any other profession, the women who teach and care for young children (there are few men in the field) have an insider's vocabulary and a distinctive way of talking about their work. Those who direct publicly funded centers inevitably absorb a technical jargon that comes from dealing with the bureaucracy of multiple government agencies. I had counted on my background in early childhood education as an entree to the centers. I soon found that center directors, like most other East Urbanites, had reasons to resist outsider investigation and to regard me, at least initially, with wariness.

One of the first groups I had contacted in East Urban was the Central Day Care Services, Inc., an organization of day care directors and social service administrators concerned with expanding and improving child care services. I arranged to attend a meeting of the group, and we talked about how I might reach parents who use relatives and neighbors for child care. We were at a point of agreement that a good way to begin would be to talk to parents on center waiting lists, when Donna, the director of the Elm Street center, arrived. Even though she was half an hour late, she quickly assumed a leadership role and squelched the waiting list plan by pointing out that parents might color their answers to my questions in order to improve their chances of being accepted into the center and of moving up higher on the list. Donna was authoritative and succeeded in convincing us that she knew best. We had been naive, she implied, to think that an interviewer could be allowed to freely contact parents. Such interference could only disrupt the system and possibly open the door for favoritism. She made me feel that I had much to learn about the everyday realities of running a day care center in East Urban.

I had the impression that Donna was constantly on her guard, and I was not surprised to learn that she would not agree to be interviewed until she received a letter for her files explaining the purpose of my visit. On my first try at setting up an appointment, Donna answered through her secretary that she would not be available for several weeks, until after Christmas vacation. When I telephoned again, after a month, she agreed to meet with me but said I should telephone the other two directors of publicly funded centers so that I could meet with all three at once. I explained that I would prefer to meet each director separately at her own center, but Donna insisted that we all meet together in her office. I was afraid Donna would dominate the interview and inhibit the others. Nevertheless I dutifully set up the appointment with the other two directors—Ruth of the Johnson School center and Ana of the La Casa center. On the appointed day, however, they didn't show up, and I had Donna to myself.

ELM STREET DAY CARE: SOME GUARDED ANSWERS

Donna's appearance surprised me. Dressed in a blue sweatshirt decorated with a silver lightning bolt and matching sweatpants stuffed into what looked like ponyskin boots with feather decorations, she did not fulfill my picture of how a day care director was "supposed" to look. I have come to expect directors to dress in a casual, practical fashion that suits their work with children but also proclaims a kind of sincerity that precludes personal vanity.

Donna greeted me cordially but said she couldn't talk to me in her office because it was being sprayed for roaches. She proposed we meet instead in the outer office, but when it became apparent that the other two center directors weren't coming, she decided to move the interview to the office of Luz, the center's Hispanic family worker.

Luz was persuaded to give up her break for the interview, but agreed only after being promised that she could go home early to make up for the lost time. I was beginning to understand some of Donna's problems.

Elm Street probably draws its reputation as the center that black parents use from the fact that it is located near the projects, where most of East Urban's African-American population lives. Although Elm Street has more black families than the other two public centers, over half of its enrollment is Hispanic. Elm Street is the oldest center, started in 1969 with federal model cities money. Unlike the other two subsidized centers, which were located first in churches and then in public schools, Elm Street was designed as a day care center within a community center offering a variety of social services.

Elm Street cares for children from 6 months to school age, and its present enrollment is 10 infants and toddlers, 64 preschoolers from two to five, and 62 after-school children. When I asked about what kinds of parents use the center, Donna advised me to get a copy of the Department of Social Services guideline book. When I asked about fees, she rattled off the telephone number I should call to ask for a copy of the fee scale. She obviously felt that she would rather have me consult an official manual than ask her questions about specific cases. "There is so much to read," she explained. "Like if the woman isn't married and the man lives with her—is that included?"

When I later obtained copies of the documents from the state I learned that children are admitted according to six priorities. Fifteen percent of children admitted must come from priorities one and two, which are for children in need of protective services and for children referred as being at risk or in need of special services. Priority three is for children from families in which day care is necessary to prevent placement of the child outside the home. Priorities four and five are for children of parents who work or go to school. Priority six is for all other families.

Luz described these categories slightly differently. She said approximately 18 children should be from "referred" parents in priority one or two. Priorities three through six she described by a variety of school and work eligibilities, as follows:

> Priority three would be those parents who are categorized as part-time working parents but at the same time are also students, so they are referred to us by a school, say in an internship. They have so much to go before they can actually work full-time. They still may live on welfare and only receive a stipend for child care. Our fourth

category are full-time working parents. Fifth would be that parent who is a student and receiving welfare. Last priority is welfare.

A mother, to qualify for this day care, must be a working parent or going back to school. We make allowance for a teenage mom because sometimes they need day care. But a welfare parent who has come off the street and says, "I take welfare and I don't do anything," we feel that they're capable of taking care of their own. We do accept welfare parents, but we give them a month to find a job. If they don't find a job in a month, that's it. Termination. Parents must produce pay stubs. We re-determine every six months.

Listening to Luz, I could see how difficult the job of establishing eligibility would be in a community with so many needy families. Donna explained that she always has a waiting list, and I could sympathize with the almost impossible job of choosing among parents in desperate need of day care. I could also understand the reasons for Donna's guarded attitude toward me. She was in a ticklish position between the local community of parents and the state-level administrative bureaucracy. She gained her authority for making decisions from the rules of the bureaucracy, but in fact she was called on to make many on-the-spot decisions for cases not described by the rules. In this position she did not welcome outsider scrutiny of her already oversensitive administrative process.

Donna described the care at her center as "above adequate," but hastened to add (perhaps for Luz's benefit) that her staff was "superb" and "quite dedicated" despite their pay, which "is less than a zookeeper." She concluded, "The care is very nice." And then to illustrate her point, she added, "The kids enjoy each other's company. They want to be as close as possible, sleeping back to back and on top of one another." (When Donna later described how tight her space was, it appeared that such piling up might be not so much a matter of affection as of necessity. In any case, it seemed to me an odd way of documenting the center's quality.)

Donna saw the main drawbacks of the center as those of space. The children are too crowded, and the place is difficult to keep clean, particularly since the budget for maintenance is small. She worries that the infants in the infant and toddler program may be overwhelmed by the presence nearby of older children who, she feels, do not have adequate play space. "I wish we were able to get more funding and bigger classrooms," she said, "and less children."

I asked Donna about the relative merits of her program compared with nonregulated care in homes. She answered that Elm Street is less

expensive than babysitters, especially considering the hours of care—
from 7:30 in the morning until 5:30 at night—and the breakfast, lunch,
and snack that are provided. But she also saw the advantages of family
day care.

> I'm a parent and I can see both sides. I really think day care is
> terrific. But you have four teachers with 34 kids in the class-
> room. If you can get the same kind of care with good quality,
> small home-based care where the kids can go out and play, and
> you strolled or gave more individualized attention—which you
> do when you have family day care—that's fine too.

Donna does not take infants younger than 6 months and has no
desire to lower this age limit. "We don't want to take a very, very
young, fragile child in the classroom where we have toddlers as well. I
think it's an awful responsibility for the teachers to have to deal with a
6- or 8-week-old and 2-year-olds when they're all together in one
class."

Because the infant and toddler program is limited to 10 places,
most of the children at the center have been previously cared for by
their mothers at home or "usually by relatives or close neighbors."
Donna said she could not generalize about the quality of this care
because "each family is different," but neither she nor Luz had heard
of cases where children were neglected while in the care of babysitters.

When I asked what kinds of reasons parents had for changing
from relative care to center-based care for their children, Donna gave
a recent example of a single working mother living with her mother,
who stayed at home to take care of her grandchild. When a center
place became available, the family was grateful because it meant that
both women, the mother and grandmother, could be employed, thus
providing the household with two incomes.

I was eager to use Donna's center as an avenue to parents who had
used other forms of care, and I proposed interviewing parents about
what kind of arrangements they had made before being accepted into
the center. Donna said I should put my request in writing and explain
that my project was not sponsored by the center. She wanted it made
very clear to parents that no expenses connected with the research
were "coming from their children's toys or our funding." I wrote the
letter immediately and sent it to Elm Street, but I never heard from
Donna again.

JOHNSON SCHOOL DAY CARE: OPINIONS FROM AN OUTSIDER

An architectural historian might be delighted by the 70-year-old Johnson School, with its solid red brick exterior, its terrazzo floors and brass hardware, and its dedication plaque in the entryway extolling the virtues of public education; but to the staff of the day care center housed within, the school is a disastrous setting, unwieldy and outmoded. They complain about the lack of security, the noise and roughness of older students, and the large, high-ceilinged rooms as unsuited to the activities of very young children.

I had been told that the center was down the hall to the left on the first floor. Since no one was around, I made my way to the center's door, where a small, unattended table held a book for visitors to sign in, presumably on a voluntary basis. Inside, I found a small reception area with several staff people, a couple of children, and a ringing telephone. In contrast to the outside school corridor, polished to shining clean perfection without a child in sight, the day care center was a vital place—crowded, cluttered, cheerful, noisy, and friendly.

Ruth, the director of Johnson, is a comfortable-looking woman, plump enough to provide a soft lap or shoulder for a child needing sympathy. This is Ruth's second year at the center, and although she is of Italian heritage she considers herself an outsider to the East Urban scene. She grew up in an all-white, affluent, suburban community, and this is her first job in funded day care; she previously worked in private programs. "I'm an observer of how it works" is how she described herself and, in contrast to Donna, gave her impressions of the town candidly and without hesitation.

Ruth stated forthrightly what I had gathered indirectly during my interview with Donna—that dealing as a day care director with East Urban's various factions was not an easy job. Ruth began by giving her impressions of the town.

> It's an urban area, but it's a small town. A lot of people know each other, and it's accessible because of its size. But that's also its problem, because it's almost like an incestuous relationship where everyone knows everybody's business. And it's a very political city, which causes great problems. Even in day care. There's pressure from political people. "Can you get this kid in? Can you get that kid in? Can you put this child at the top of the list?" And we can't, because we have a strict waiting list. And we really 100% try to keep that waiting list. But you get a

lot of pressure. At least I do. And then if there's a problem it gets magnified. It's almost like the grapevine. If there's a day care problem, or any problem in people's lives, anywhere, it gets magnified. That's the good part of East Urban, and that's the bad part of East Urban.

Despite Johnson's reputation as the center that white parents use when they use subsidized care, it is mostly Hispanic—75 to 80%. Almost all of the rest of the children are Indian, with "some" white children and a "very small smattering" of black children, who are (in contrast to those at Elm Street) from two-parent families at the high end of the income scale. Although the white parents are small in number, Ruth says they give her the most difficulty. "Anytime when the parent comes in here angry and wants to take the child out, it's almost invariably a white child," she says. The white parents do not complain so much about the presence of Hispanic children as they do about the Indian families, who represent the most recent arrivals in the neighborhood.

> The white people who come here, whenever there's any little problem, they will come up to me and tell me that they know this center isn't really any good because look at the kind of people that are here. "I'm taking my kid out because there was head lice, I'm taking my kid out because the teachers speak Spanish. I'm taking my kid out because I don't want her to be with these people." It's really hard. They have a prejudice against the Indians. Anytime there is some sort of trouble, they always use the reference of the makeup of the center. They only use the center if they have to, if it's a must for them. They always bring it up. "If I didn't have to, I wouldn't have my kid here."

Johnson has an enrollment of 13 infants starting at 3 months, 80 children from ages two to five, and 17 older after-school children. The wait for a place can last more than a year, with infant slots in particular demand. When infants are admitted, however, many stay for only 2 or 3 months before their mothers take them out again. Ruth has tried to account for "this paradoxical thing" and has concluded that it is teenage mothers, who "really are babies themselves" and "don't appreciate" the service, who use the center for only a short time and then decide to leave their children with relatives instead.

Most parents at Johnson earn $15,000 a year or less, usually for factory work, and pay about $40 a month for the care. Seventy-five percent are single mothers, most of whom live with their parents, who help them financially because the mothers receive little support from the children's fathers. A few higher-earning families use the after-school program, which, because it is not subsidized, is more expensive ($75 a month) than lower-income families can afford. But professional parents, says Ruth, "are put off by the style of the center. This is a big school, and they don't equate day care with this type of a center. They want something real cute. That's not here. This is nitty-gritty kind of stuff."

Ruth says that most of the children have been with a maternal relative—a grandmother, an aunt, or a sister—before coming to the center. "All the family groups here are very close-knit with the exception of the Orientals, who are usually only here to study for a little while and then go back. The Indian people are very close and the Spanish people are very close. They have large extended families living in the same house, and friends that are almost like family. So they manage."

Asked for her opinion of the quality of informal care, Ruth answered, "I don't think informal care by relatives is bad, especially if it's a consistent and loving caretaker. Until the child is 2-and-a-half I think it's probably preferable. I know I shouldn't say that, but I feel that it's okay. But after 2-and-a-half I think the children are better off in a center." Ruth can see, however, why parents may resist center-based care.

> There are some responsibilities with having the child in the center that you don't have at home. You must bring them by 9:00. You must pick them up at 5:30 or there's no one here to take care. You are going to be scrutinized by outsiders, often people not of the same type that you are, so they may not understand your ways and your culture. The children will be eating foods that are foreign to them, foods that maybe the parents don't like or don't agree with. They'll be introduced to a different way, an institutionalized way of doing things. Not every parent thinks that's a good thing, and maybe they're right.

Fifteen percent of Johnson's enrollment, as at Elm Street, are children with "special needs." Although the center staff includes a parent educator and a social worker ("a person who can deal with the bureaucracy in a humane manner"), not everyone who needs help is willing to seek it through the center. Ruth says that parents who may be coping with family problems of drugs, alcohol, or child abuse are "terribly afraid" of the state's Department of Social Services.

> They think that the department will take their children away. And they are right in some ways—the department is always on the lookout, and they should be. But the parents see it as an intrusion into their personal lives. When things get hot, a lot of times the parents just pull the child out. You have to be very careful. You have to know just how much pressure to put on so that you don't lose the child. If you lose the child, you can't help the child.

Ruth does the best she can. "I never want people to come here and feel this is just another welfare office where nobody knows you and you just look like another person. I really try to get to know every parent's name, every child's—really talk to them a lot to make them feel as comfortable as possible."

Like Donna, Ruth sees her space as her biggest problem and her staff as her greatest asset.

> This setting does not lend itself to day care. I think it's the worst you could do. It's spread out on two floors. It's in an old building where there's asbestos, where there are people coming in and out. It's cold, drafty, and dank on days like today. But the people on the staff have a lot of heart. They really love the children. They are trying to make something out of nothing.

One of the things Ruth is most proud of is how her staff, with her encouragement, have taken courses in early childhood education. The center will pay for courses if staff members earn marks of C or better, and everyone so far is getting Bs. Since no one has a car, they must take two buses to night classes after a long day at the center. Ruth is very proud of their progress and cheers their successes. She hopes to improve her program by having a better-trained staff and so encourages them to "stretch."

> The more education they have, the more they can stretch. We're creating a new curriculum. In the beginning it was very frustrating for some of the teachers, and they cried—really cried— "I can't do this. I don't even know what you're talking about.

I'm trying so hard and I haven't reached your expectations."
And I have to say, "Yes, you are trying very hard, and I appre-
ciate that, but this is not what I want. I want more from you."
It's very hard for people, but it's so good for the kids.

Ruth is aware that her ideas for a new curriculum are foreign not
only to her staff but to many of the parents. When I asked if the
improvements were what parents wanted, she spoke with the forceful-
ness of someone who feels sure of her ground.

I don't care what they want. I don't even think they do like it.
And I really don't care, because they are tired. They only want
a decent, safe place, which is the first thing. You have to have a
safe place. But they don't know what the children need. They
think they need to know the alphabet at 2 years old. So I can't
go by what the parents think is right; I have to go by what I
know is right. What they think and what I think are two different things.

When I asked more specifically about what she thought was best,
Ruth first answered that I should read the center's official mission
statement. But then she began to speak from her own convictions,
summing up a philosophy of child developmental theory as set within
the tangled web of East Urban's diversity.

I want the children to be treated as individuals as much as possible in such a setting—allow for what the age of the child is,
and their development, and what they can accomplish. Give
them an opportunity to reach their potential. And then teach
them the standard things as you go—socialization, how to get
along with other children, introduce new foods, accent their
culture. Because this is a multicultural center. We try to do in-
ternational things, very much Hispanic, while teaching the
main culture. Because unless they absorb the main culture and
learn English they will never get out of the economic situation
that most of the people are in. I tell Hispanic parents it is very
important for them to love their own culture. They should encourage that. And they should learn their own language. But
they must also learn English and learn English ways. Because
they will never make it if they don't. There are some people
who are willing to listen to that. And some people who don't
even care.

LA CASA: PRIDE OF HERITAGE

Like the Johnson School center, the La Casa center is located in what I
had come to regard as a typical East Urban school—solid, brick,
formidable, and seemingly indestructible. As in the Johnson School,
the hallways were quiet and empty. It may be that the solidity of the
walls and a policy of closed classroom doors account for the calm, but
it also seems likely that this is a school where silence is golden and
noise spells trouble. When I asked a custodian the way to the center, he
pointed down the hall.

The day care center office was crowded with two desks almost
side by side. At one desk sat the school secretary, Angela, who greeted
me. The other desk was turned away from the door. When I had
introduced myself and explained that I had an appointment with Ana,
the director, Angela indicated that the other woman was Ana. Lacking
a private office, Ana sat with her back to visitors. Angela, thin and
pretty, wore an attractive dress and a gold necklace that spelled out
her name. Ana, a calm, capable woman with a dignified manner, was
dressed more somberly in a dark blouse and pants. Both are Hispanic.
Ana, like Donna and Ruth, lives outside East Urban. Angela lives in
East Urban and, having started as a paraprofessional, has been with
the center since its organization over 10 years ago. Ana was not eager
to be interviewed but slowly warmed to the process as she described
La Casa's program, to which she is obviously devoted. Angela, at the
beginning of the interview, spoke so softly as to be almost inaudible,
but as the conversation went on she became more animated and less
guarded than Ana.

La Casa began under the sponsorship of a Hispanic church as a
service for Latino families and was first located in the church basement. Although I had heard from parents who had their children in
the center when it was located in the church basement that the facilities there were poor and hard to keep clean, Ana looks back on those
years with nostalgia. When the center was in the church it was "our
space," not subject to the restrictions of being in a Board of Education
building.

La Casa is one of the very few agencies in East Urban organized
specifically for Hispanic families. It is bilingual in the sense that most
of the teachers speak both English and Spanish, although English is the
principal language. All children are taught songs in Spanish, and Hispanic children who don't know English are addressed in both lan-
guages. Although the enrollment was originally only Hispanic families,
the center is now more integrated, which Ana sees as an improvement.

"I think it's very important for children to know that there are kids who are different from themselves, other colors and races," she says. The center now has 47 children—mostly Hispanic, but also Indians (called "Hindus" at La Casa), Asians whose parents are studying at a local technical college, a few non-Hispanic whites, and one non-Hispanic black. Some of the Indian and Asian children arrive at the center knowing only their own language and are taught both English and some Spanish. "They pick it up fast, in 3 or 4 months," Ana said.

This year, for the first time in its history, the center is under-enrolled, with less than its capacity of 60 children. Ana attributed the shrinking enrollment to a decline in East Urban's Hispanic population, although families at the center now come from Colombia, Costa Rica, Uruguay, the Dominican Republic, Cuba, Peru, El Salvador, Paraguay, and Chile, in addition to Puerto Rico. Ana blames increased rents for driving the Hispanic population she formerly served to other locations. Most of the parents, she said, are factory workers earning less than $5 an hour. She estimated that about a third were single-parent families and that most of them had three or four children.

Ana said the parents in La Casa want "learning" for their children, and they expect them to be taught "the colors, the letters, the numbers, how to write their names. Some want them to learn to speak English." The La Casa staff is sympathetic to these aims and works hard to prepare La Casa children for public school. It angers Ana when her "graduates" are assumed by public school teachers to lack preparation for kindergarten and are required to repeat what they have already learned at La Casa, or are placed in bilingual classes on the assumption that because they have a Hispanic name they do not know English.

Ana puts a great deal of effort into letting parents know what happens at the center. She assumes that her program will meet with parental approval and sends home descriptions of each week's activities, blocked out into time schedules and lesson plans. On Visiting Day parents participate in the children's activities and are encouraged to ask questions. A bulletin board at the entrance to the office keeps parents abreast of current happenings. To avoid misunderstandings about punishment, parents are asked to sign a statement from the center's board of directors about discipline, and teachers are required to follow its guidelines. Ana is proud of the parents' active participation at La Casa. "We've never had a problem with our parents' meetings," she said with satisfaction. "We've always had a good turnout."

La Casa accepts children from age two to five. Ana is "dying" for an infant program and would like to add an after-school program as well to increase her enrollment. She said there is a demand for infant care because "more women want to go to work. At one time they wanted to stay home at least until the child was old enough to go to school. Now it's the economic need that they have to get to work right away—high rents, food, clothing, everything."

Most parents, she said, have had their children with babysitters—"friends, relatives, mothers, sisters, a close friend, or somebody who knows someone who babysits"—before coming to La Casa. Some of the single mothers, who have stayed at home on welfare, enter school-to-work programs when child care becomes available. Others switch from sitters to the center because the fees are lower. "I've heard people say, 'My babysitter is very good, but she's too expensive,'" Ana explained, "or, 'She left to go to Puerto Rico,' or 'The children aren't learning,' or whatever. The reasons vary."

Both Ana and Angela, as working mothers themselves, have histories of using a combination of relative care and center-based care when their own children were young. When Angela worked as a sales clerk, she used her sister-in-law as a week-long babysitter, dropping her child off on Monday and picking him up on Friday. Angela began using center-based care when she took a job in a day care center herself, keeping the same hours. Ana had a similar arrangement with her mother, who took over the complete care of both of Ana's children on a weekly basis, keeping them from Monday to Friday. Ana's commute to East Urban and the night meetings required by her position as director of the center made daily pickups too difficult. She eventually moved the older child to a day care center, but the younger one stayed with the grandmother during the week until he was ready for first grade.

After we had finished the interview, I asked Ana if I might tour the center. I could see why she, like Ruth, considered space one of her main problems. The school was built with a stage at one side of the gym so that it could double as an auditorium. La Casa's kitchen had been carved out of the backstage area. The four groups of children were in two former classrooms, two groups to each room, with low partitions dividing the rooms. When I observed, the children were napping (or silently awake) in darkened rooms, and even with a reduced enrollment the space was crowded with cots.

As Ana walked with me down the hallway on my way out, I asked her if the program was in danger of being phased out. I had heard that the school might change to a vocational high school, and Ana confirmed this. When I suggested that maybe children on waiting lists at Johnson School and Elm Street might be given the extra places at La Casa, Ana replied that she had already asked for names of parents on the waiting lists but had not been given them. Perhaps, she said, people don't want to put their children in a center with a Hispanic name. When I jokingly suggested she might do better with something a little cuter, like "Wee Tots," she answered seriously that La Casa was proud of its history and would never change its name.

COMMUNITY SERVICES: FIGHTING CITY HALL

The agency in charge of East Urban's subsidized child care centers is the Department of Community Services (whose building also houses the Elm Street center). Marjory, who monitors the programs, is a Born and Raised second-generation Italian, whose story I have already described in Chapter 2. In addition to day care programs, she supervises senior citizen centers and other federally funded programs that require a match of local dollar contributions from the community where they are located. It is Marjory's job "to monitor how programs spend the money we give them and to give technical assistance if they have any problems."

Marjory's "mission in life" is to build new day care centers on city-owned land. She described how the Johnson School and La Casa centers had started in churches, only to be displaced into public schools, which "are not the proper place for day care programs."

They're not secure. Anyone can come in off the street. You have a terrible noise problem because you have the whole school coming down to the gym, which is right next to where the kids are. A child could easily get lost if you are not really careful. They are big buildings, and the outside doors are open to walk in or out. There should be more glass, so that you can see in and out of the classroom to what's happening—so parents can walk in unannounced and see what's happening with the children. These are wonderful programs. Given the proper sites they would be excellent.

Not that it had been simple to move the centers into the schools. Marjory recounted her battles with the Board of Education to get them to understand that the programs had to be from at least 8:00 until 6:00 for the benefit of working parents.

I had to explain that this is totally different from a nursery situation where mothers just want to get the child used to being

with other children. I went to the Board, but they give you a
hard time. They're in their own little world, and they don't like
invaders. They didn't understand—now they do because I
fought so hard—that this is not an after-school for an hour or
two. It's a full-day, full-year program for working parents.

As the limitations of the public school sites become ever more
apparent, Marjory has escalated her drive toward building a center.
She located a suitable site, but federal funding went toward affordable
housing instead. When the city procured $5 million for senior citizens it
decided to use the site for a senior citizen center. Marjory's office then
produced a "funding package" application to combine day care with
senior citizen housing.

We thought it was an excellent idea—use two ground floors for
day care and house seniors above, with separate entrances and
so forth. The only allowable other interest in the building for
senior citizens was if it would benefit the seniors. I thought it
would benefit them. However, the people in charge meant a
dry cleaners or something. Not a day care center.

Day care advocates were outraged. A state-level day care official
told me later that the decision was a "very, very slimy, snaky move" on
the city's part. She said the reason was that "kids don't vote" and that
"people feel sorry for old people." They get into sentimental issues.
One out of every four senior citizens is in senior citizen housing, but
where do the kids go? The city of East Urban says it cares about its
children, but it's not a high priority."
    Besides lacking space, funded centers are over-enrolled, the offi-
cial explained, because centers must have 87% attendance to be reim-
bursed. To guard against loss of funding through absences, centers
over-enroll. When I asked the official to explain La Casa's under-
enrollment she gave me an explanation that reflected on East Urban's
ethnic politics. First she said that the "word is going out" that Ana
might lose her space. But she also commented that Ana lacks the
political skill to defend her position. According to the official, Ana
"doesn't know how to reach out through her Board to pressure the
town. She panics, and she thinks, 'This town hates Hispanics. We're
going to be out on the street.'" Like others who deal with Hispanic
parents in East Urban, the official commented on their lack of political
power. Because La Casa is Hispanic-sponsored, she said, its Board is
"less aggressive" than that of Johnson School, which is seen as "dy-

namic" in contrast to the "more provincial" attitude at La Casa. The differences between the two centers are so great that when a merger was suggested at the proposed new site, the centers said they would not move if they had to join together. The solution would have been to have separate quarters and entrances for the two centers at the same site.

Not only was Marjory worried about finding additional space for her day care programs, with all the political maneuvering that would require, but she was also concerned about the quality of the staff in the centers she monitors.

> The staff is not paid very much in our funded programs, so you don't get the top of the applicants and there is a very big turnover. Many of the teachers are on waiting lists for public schools. If we could offer them sufficient pay we would have a much better program. We can't offer the benefits that you get from teaching or office work or whatever. If you are a single parent and head of household and you have children, it's very important to have coverage. If you are working in a day care center—unless you are extremely dedicated—and an offer comes up with better pay and benefits, you are going to take it. Then the day care center has to look for someone else who is waiting to get into that bracket as well. You lose really good people.

When I asked Marjory about the small number of Born and Raised families using licensed day care, she answered that the private day care centers in East Urban are preferable to the public ones, which are "overcrowded and don't offer the same kind of things the private sector would." She mentioned "dance lessons" and "lots of field trips," as well as "less children, a nicer place, and a higher paid staff," as advantages of private programs, and said, "I think everybody would prefer to have their child in a private center." But, she added, the cost was prohibitive for most Born and Raised parents—"a large portion of your salary would go to child care."

The families "who take advantage of the day care centers," she said, are the Hispanics, Indians, and blacks of low- to moderate-income families. She explained that the services go to parents on welfare as well as to working parents. "If the child is in crisis, or if the mother is in counseling, or there is abusive behavior—then those children have top priority to be placed in one of our day care programs to give the mother that time away from the child."

According to Marjory, different kinds of parents use public centers for different reasons. Hispanic parents "prefer to have grandma watch the child—they are closely knit and family-oriented. So they are eligible for all of the programs, with little or no payment. So when they have to, they do take advantage of them." Indians and Asians, who are apt to be on the higher income end of the fee scale, put their children in centers as a form of early education, particularly to learn English.

Publicly funded centers are "wait listed" with 50 to 100 families on each list, according to Marjory (this may have been the case until this year, when La Casa had empty places). She saw the need for more infant programs but said that even though money is now available for these programs, there is no suitable place to be found in East Urban. "A few years back," she said, "people didn't go back to work when they had an infant, but they do today. That's the parent we have to look at very soon."

Even though Marjory is working to expand her funded programs and particularly to increase the services for infants, she personally dissociates herself from this kind of care.

> I am still from the old school. If you can afford to stay at home with an infant, I think that is best. At least for the first year. You need that bonding. Next best is with relatives until school age, when they are used to being with strangers and other children. Then after school for an hour or two in a center would not be so horrendous.

TINY TOTS: ONE OF A CHAIN

The first private day care center I visited was Tiny Tots, which is located in the quaint outbuildings of a nineteenth-century church built in the Gothic style—a far cry from the public school settings of subsidized centers. I first learned about Tiny Tots during an interview with a Born and Raised teacher who runs an after-school program in a nearby Catholic school. Years ago, she had taught Tiny Tots' director, Laura, as a student in the same Catholic school. Discussing how family life in the neighborhood had changed over the years, the teacher told me with more wonderment than condemnation that Laura now ran a nearby "day care" where parents left even tiny babies, making up their cribs and leaving them for a full day.

When I telephoned her from the school, Laura generously agreed to see me immediately. After welcoming me into her tiny office, she explained that Tiny Tots is part of a chain of day care centers whose headquarters are in another state. The chain sent a proposal to East Urban's hospital and gained its sponsorship through an agreement to offer hospital employees a reduced rate for child care. Tiny Tots has been open for 3 years. Laura herself, carefully groomed and in business clothes, appeared more like a corporate executive than a person who worked in a classroom with children.

Tiny Tots offers drop-in, hourly, part-time, and full-time care from 7:00 a.m. to 6:30 p.m. Although its capacity is 80, the present enrollment is 65 children, ages 2 months to 10 years. Fees for infant and toddlers are $4 an hour, or $85 a week; fees for preschoolers are $3.50 and hour, or $64 a week. Most of the staff comes from East Urban, some lured by free child care as a benefit. (Under state laws, publicly funded centers do not allow staff members to have their children at the same site where they work.) Three of the center's staff of 13 are certified teachers.

Laura estimates that only about half of the families in her program are from East Urban. The rest are parents from nearby suburban towns who drop off their children on their way to work in the nearby City. Laura, herself Born and Raised and a product of the local parochial schools, gave me her impression of the professional middle-class parents who use her center—"the career people, the kind who don't want a funded center." Laura feels that these full-time working parents "put their guilt" on her center. It is the fathers of infants rather than the mothers, she has found to her surprise, who ask the most questions.

> They're over-concerned and worried. One calls every day to ask questions about the baby. What did he eat? How is he feeling? The fathers are the ones who check out the center. We never hear from the mothers. Some mothers don't even come to look at the center before they leave the babies here. Now it's the fathers that are concerned about diaper changing and what the baby eats. It's because of the new roles. The women are involved in their careers. That's new for them, and they're concentrating on that. The father is new to the mother role.

I saw only one classroom at Tiny Tots and it was empty. Located on the first floor, it was high-ceilinged with large windows and was well equipped with play materials. Other classrooms and the infant program were located on the second floor, but I was not invited to tour. The church buildings had been renovated for day care use, using funds from the day care chain (Tiny Tots is its ninth center); children were cared for in a trailer on the church property until the renovations were completed.

Laura gave me a copy of "policies and procedures" for parents enrolling their children in any center of the chain. Among them was the stipulation that a service charge of $15 would be assessed for any check that was returned, and that cash must be paid in full and immediately for the child to remain in the center. For the following 3 months, penalized parents would be required to pay in cash. These directives are instructive about the difficulties that private centers encounter even from relatively affluent parents who are unable or unwilling to pay their fees.

THE LEARNING CENTER: SUBURBAN PARENTS

East Urban's other private day care center, the Learning Center, is also located in a church, but its facilities are not as attractive as those of Tiny Tots. Searching for its entrance in the pouring rain, I entered the church's side yard, which was small and dismal, with a few drenched pieces of play equipment left on the small plot of grass between two concrete paths. I made my way to a door straight ahead but soon realized that the day care entrance was down some stairs to my left at the basement level. To me, this was an even less attractive spot than the funded day care centers. Inside a small entryway a glass panel allowed Jeanne, the director, to screen entering visitors and buzz them in from her office.

Jeanne's office was scruffy and disorganized. One of the ceiling tiles was loose and the walls needed paint. She explained a large jumble of children's books on top of a cabinet by saying that all the teachers use them constantly. When I had telephoned Jeanne for an interview, she had been hesitant, and she began our talk by making it clear that she was not the owner of the center, just the director. Like Laura, she is from a moderate-income background and also had risen to her administrative level from the job of teacher. (In fact, she was still responsible for one of the four groups of children at the center.)

The Learning Center was founded 3 years earlier when parents from nearby suburbs who had moved to East Urban decided to start a day care center "because they wanted good quality care and there wasn't any here." The parents located the church basement space and organized the center as a branch of two programs already established in suburban locations.

Jeanne described the parents in the center as "in transit," moving from the suburbs to East Urban or vice versa. "A lot move back to the suburbs when their children get older," she said, "to better public schools." The Learning Center now has an enrollment of 50 children ranging in age from 2 months to 4 years. It is operating at much less than its capacity of 80 and recently lost six families who decided to move from East Urban.

Jeanne refers to the parents in her center as "yuppies." "The majority are career-oriented," she says. "Most mothers work. There are only a few who don't. These families work in the City, but they don't want to pay City taxes so they live here." When I asked if any of the parents were born in East Urban, she answered, "No, they're basically career-oriented" (as though being born in East Urban and having a career were mutually exclusive categories). She mentally reviewed her parent roster and said that although one parent is an actor and several are in publishing, "most are business." The center has had a few Hispanic children, an occasional Indian child, and two black children—one the child of a fashion model and the other the child of a minister.

During our interview Jeanne was interrupted by the telephone and talked to someone who obviously could not afford the $79 she quoted as a weekly fee. "This is not a Title Twenty program," she said pointedly, referring to the federal day care subsidy, "you know what I mean?" She suggested the caller try Head Start, La Casa, and Elm Street for possible openings. I asked Jeanne what alternatives there were in child care for Learning Center parents. "They have in-home care," she answered. "They call them nannies."

Jeanne, like Laura, was impressed by the roles the fathers of children in her center play, but her analysis was different. She said fathers do most of the dropping off and picking up "to give their wives a break." At her center, she reported, mothers and fathers both take part in making the arrangements for care, "It's a joint decision," she explained, "because it's joint money."

Jeanne complained that "hardly anybody comes to parent meetings, because of their careers. They come home late and don't want to go out at night. They want to spend their evening time with their kids." When she tried to organize a picnic for parents and children, nobody signed up. I asked Jeanne if she thought these were "good parents." Her first response was, "Yes, the children know their ABCs and they have great toys." She paused as though thinking this over and then expanded, "The parents are very caring, they work with their children."

Before leaving, I asked to see Jeanne's group of children (I had the feeling that if I hadn't asked she would have hustled me out the door). The four groups of children—nine infants, nine toddlers, thirteen 2- and 3-year-olds, and Jeanne's eighteen 3- and 4-year-olds—were divided by low partitions in the darkened basement. Jeanne's group was nearing the end of its hour-and-a-half nap. As Jeanne looked over the partition, several children sat up on their mats, fully awake, but Jeanne told them to lie back down. In the background an infant squalled steadily as it had during the last 5 minutes of our interview.

THE ECONOMICS OF LICENSED CARE

In East Urban, day care centers are widely divided along economic lines into two distinctive groups—subsidized and private. In publicly subsidized centers, fees average around $10 a week. In private day care centers, fees are as high as $85 a week. As a result, minority and single-parent families constitute a high proportion of the families served by publicly funded centers. The only families who can afford the private day care centers are those earning relatively high incomes (for East Urban), and they tend to be two-parent families where one or both parents hold white-collar or professional career jobs. With few exceptions, these parents are white.

Born and Raised parents are not likely to earn enough to send their children to the private centers, but many earn too much to be eligible for subsidized child care. They are caught in the middle—another reason to postpone maternal employment until children are old enough to enter full-day school. But even if Born and Raised parents are eligible for subsidized care and need it, they may seek informal child care arrangements instead to avoid using subsidized care.

WHO GOES TO WHICH CENTER

Because of the priorities set by the state Department of Social Services, subsidized centers take children in special need of care—those who are at risk, or who need special or protective services, or who otherwise might be placed outside the home. The large number of such children reflects not only damaging social conditions but also increased surveillance by public officials. This overseeing by the Department of Social Services has become so much an accepted part of subsidized care that some poor parents regard it as the only way to get their children into center-based care. And once children are in subsidized care, their parents, as reported at the Johnson School center, may be ever mindful of having to "pass inspection."

The presence of so many children identified as "in special need," together with the large numbers of minority children, acts as a deterrent to Born and Raised participation in subsidized child care. Born and Raised families pride themselves on maintaining their ethnic identity—an identity that depends in part on differentiating themselves from those who must rely on welfare services. Because the economic circumstances of the Born and Raised are so often precarious, maintaining themselves as different from those "below" becomes especially important. To the extent that subsidized day care is viewed as a welfare service for single minority mothers with troubled or neglected children, it becomes less attractive to those, like the Born and Raised (and many minority parents), whose pride is based on distancing themselves from that very same population.

Even within the realm of publicly funded day care, each of the three centers has a distinct reputation. Although very few parents I talked to could describe the whole array of center-based care, parents described the reputations of those centers they had heard of. Although all three subsidized centers have 60% or more Hispanic families, each has a reputation for one kind of family. La Casa, where the director and staff are all Spanish-speaking and whose origin was in a Spanish-speaking church, is known as Hispanic. Johnson School, despite its small white enrollment, is known as the center for white parents when they do use funded day care. Elm Street is known for its black families who come from the nearby projects, even though they are outnumbered by Hispanic families. It seems that day care centers, like public schools, are identified by the ethnic and racial predominance of the neighborhood in which they are located. These divisions are so strong that Elm Street's board refused to consider merging with La Casa under a projected plan to relocate to improved quarters. Despite the fact that La Casa is under-enrolled while Elm Street and Johnson School have a shortage of places, waiting lists are not shared.

The two private day care centers in East Urban, Tiny Tots and the Learning Center, attract parents of a very different sort from the subsidized centers. These parents earn relatively high salaries, are in predominantly two-parent families, and come from a transient population of career people. They are newcomers who have moved from the suburbs to East Urban to be within easy commuting distance of the City, where they are employed in career positions but where housing is more costly and taxes are higher. As their children approach school age, they often move back to the suburbs in search of better schools and surroundings they consider more favorable for children. This mobility means that they are not apt to have relatives available to care for their children, even if they should prefer such arrangements.

Private centers are located in churches in East Urban's "best" neighborhoods, where housing is expensive and the population largely white. But the parents who use the programs are not only from the neighborhood, as most of the parents in public centers are, but from a wide surrounding area, drawn to East Urban as a way-stop en route to jobs in the City and a place to park their cars before boarding the City-bound train.

HOW CENTER DIRECTORS VIEW PARENTS

Directors in private centers described the parents in their centers in very different terms from the way directors in subsidized centers described the parents in their centers. Part of the difference was due to the relative economic positions of directors and parents. Directors of private centers earned less than the parents they provided services for, and their jobs carried less prestige than the professional career jobs of parents. Directors in subsidized centers, by contrast, occupied jobs that were more prestigious and better paying than those of the parents (although other staff positions were paid about the same as parents earned).

These differences in the backgrounds of the staff and the parents served by the centers were reflected in how center directors talked about themselves in relation to parents. In publicly funded day care centers, directors saw themselves as providing services to families in need. They described mothers on waiting lists who planned to begin working as soon as a place was available for their child. They described mothers who depended on the center not to drop them during periods of layoffs. The directors also described their centers as resources that supported families who faced problems of child abuse, poor health, inadequate housing, and poverty. They worked closely with the Department of Social Services and local community organizations concerned with social welfare. Each of these directors was professionally trained in early childhood education, but they also spoke as social workers. They saw themselves as valuable community helpers, providing quality child care to children who might not otherwise receive it.

In the private programs, directors viewed their services to parents differently. These two directors had also received professional training in early childhood education, both having come up through the ranks of classroom teaching to the position of director. Although they considered themselves more expert than the parents in terms of child development, they held a job that lacked status in the eyes of the parents they served. They assumed that families that could afford their services were financially stable. The parents, both mothers and fathers, were highly educated, were readily employable in high-paying jobs, and had prospects of rising in their careers to even better jobs and increasing salaries.

If the problems of the parents in subsidized centers were viewed as largely resulting from poverty, the problems of parents in the private programs, as described by directors, were of a different order. The one emphasized most during the interviews was the issue of time. The demands of a career prevented parents from having enough time for other things—including their children. Private program directors viewed their centers as primarily a support for parent employment. Problems revolved around how center directors responded to the guilt of families who felt themselves caught between the demands of career and being parents.

Private center directors counted on middle-class parents to provide learning experiences at home that would prepare children for preschool. In funded centers this aspect of the program was more problematical. Both Ruth at the Johnson School center and Ana at La Casa talked about how their programs prepared Hispanic children for school. Ruth struggled to reconcile her feelings that children should maintain their ethnic identity with her equally strong feelings that to succeed they must master mainstream skills, particularly learning English. She assumed a position of authority derived from a professional knowledge of child development—she felt strongly that she knew better than parents what was best for their children in terms of the center's program. Ana, Hispanic herself, was less conflicted. She assumed that if she explained her program (which also emphasized the learning of English but within a bilingual setting) to parents, they would approve. Ruth's main goal was to have an individualized, developmentally appropriate program. Ana's was to structure her program on a school model, emphasizing the early learning of letters and colors, which parents also wanted.

PUBLIC AND PRIVATE

In my short visits (which were probably longer than those given most prospective parents), I was able to gain only the most superficial impression of quality. However, on this basis it would be difficult to say why parents would consider the private centers to be of better quality than the publicly funded ones. To me, the converted classrooms of the Johnson School were no worse as a center setting than the church basement of the Learning Center. Directors in the publicly funded centers were just as qualified, if not more so, as those in the private centers, and the publicly funded directors were more articulate about the goals of their programs. If private centers were less "crowded," it was due to under-enrollment; their classrooms were actually smaller than those in the funded centers.

What appeared to differentiate the publicly funded centers from the private ones was more a matter of economics than of quality. Because the private centers charged so much more than the public ones, some parents might assume that the higher prices brought higher quality. What such assumptions overlook is that the fees paid by parents in funded programs are only a small part of the actual cost of care; the remainder of the cost is made up by government subsidy.

The other factor, of course, is that the disparate fees charged by funded and private centers effectively segregate the families who use the centers by economic class, and consequently by race and ethnicity. Children in private centers are from advantaged backgrounds, with all that implies in terms of health care, housing, and ways of raising children. Families in funded centers are beset by the problems of poverty, and their children are likely to bear these burdens in terms of poor health, behavior disorders, and learning difficulties.

If child care were offered on a universal basis with sufficient government funding to make it available to all families at a reasonable cost, would parents self-select into similar patterns of segregation by economic class? We do not know the answer, but East Urban provides some clues. Location can make a difference. Johnson School is a funded center, yet its location in a "mixed" neighborhood means that a wider variety of parents use it than the other two funded centers, which are located in neighborhoods that are predominantly poor. The proposed plans for new, more centrally located facilities might encourage a greater mix of families, but a merger has so far been resisted by center parents, who cling to their community roots as a source of identity and view their differences as a source of strength rather than as a shortcoming.

Chapter 7

Other East Urban Parents Tell Their Stories

Although I had targeted East Urban's Born and Raised families as a focus for my study, I also interviewed parents from other backgrounds. Some of these I consciously pursued as members of a different ethnic or racial group, not because they were particularly representative, but as individuals in differing circumstances whose child care choices were framed by other social contexts. I listened to family histories of successive generations, of old and new neighborhoods, of jobs held and lost, of children and their growing up, of plans for the future and remembrances of the past. These parents differed widely in the details of their family life, yet they all were coping with the basic issues of reconciling employment and child care and of weighing the advantages of one kind of care against another. In the following parent stories Brian is "American," Gita is Indian, Yolanda is Hispanic, and Patricia is African-American. The circumstances in which their families live form dramatic contrasts to each other, and yet, because they live in the same city, their individual stories are played out against a common background of the choices East Urban can offer any parent seeking a solution to the problems of child care.

BRIAN: TWO-CAREER PROFESSIONALS

My reason for interviewing Brian was to ask him about how East Urban Indians arranged for child care. As the white "American" minister of a Protestant church whose congregation was about half Indian, he had been described to me as someone who could provide information on Indian families. In the course of our interview he also described his own family's child care arrangements for their two young

children, which gave me a picture of child care in a two-career professional middle-class family.

Brian's church is on the corner of a block populated mostly by
families of German descent, many of whom are older people who
attend his church. Since East Urban's Germans were among the earli-
est immigrants, preceding both the Italians and the Puerto Ricans, they
are accepted as Born and Raised and see themselves as an established
and stable presence. Many own their houses and keep them in good
repair. As a result, this neighborhood is considered one of East Urban's
"better" sections.

Brian and his family live in the church's manse, next door to the
church. Both are handsome buildings dating from the nineteenth century. The manse is surrounded by an antique decorative iron fence
enclosing a tiny patch of ground that is the closest one can come to a
front yard in East Urban. Brian, accompanied by a police dog, answered the door and ushered me into a small vestibule. Looking
younger than his 39 years, he was thin and trim and dressed casually in
pants and a sweater.

After I had hung up my coat, Brian led me into the front parlor
where our interview would take place. Almost immediately the telephone rang, as it was to do repeatedly during my stay, and Brian went
into the next room to answer it and talk church business. As I looked
around, I was struck by how carefully the furnishings had been chosen
to reflect a life of "culture." The bench for the upright piano was
covered in needlepoint. A glass-doored bookcase displayed a new set
of an encyclopedia, a vintage set of matched works by Dickens, and
a copy of *Great Operas*. A bud vase held a single artificial rose. A
reproduction of Gainsborough's "Blue Boy" on one wall faced wedding photographs across the room. The effect was prim and neat. I
saw no signs of children.

Brian and his wife, Ellice, moved to east Urban as adults when
Brian was offered the job as minister. They both work full-time. Ellice,
who holds a Master of Social Work degree, heads a center for the
elderly. Their two daughters, one 2-and-a-half years old and the other
an infant of 2 weeks, were born in East Urban. They had placed their
older daughter in a private day care center when she was 2 months
old—the youngest allowable age—and planned to do the same with
their younger daughter. Ellice would return to work part-time when
the baby was one month old and resume full-time work when the baby
was 2 months old. Brian and Ellice were in agreement about putting
their infants in center-based care. "We discussed it early on," said

Brian, "and realized we'd both crack up if we weren't working. So there's no other solution."

Brian is aware of the contrast between his family and those of his Indian parishioners, whose infants are cared for by their mothers or other relatives. "It's a question of availability," he explained. "If we had a family with 15 adults like the Indians do, we might feel differently." He paused, then laughed and added, "But it would probably drive me crazy." As it is, care by relatives "isn't an option." Both Brian and Ellice come from small families that are now scattered. Brian's parents both hold jobs in another city. His only sister lives in another state. Ellice's parents also live far away. Both sets of grandparents disapprove of Ellice's continuing her career while her children are young. Both grandmothers stayed at home when their children were young, and they wish Ellice would quit her job to do the same. Brian resents this. "Their advice is, 'Ellice should quit working and stay home and raise the children.' *My* advice to *them* is, 'Mind your own business.'"

Brian and Ellice are completely satisfied with Tiny Tots, the private day care center they chose for their older daughter. They had heard good reports about the center from church members, paid a visit, and then enrolled their daughter. "It's a nice place and it's close," Brian explained. They have heard that the Learning Center, the other private day care center in East Urban, is "magnificent" but have never visited it. Brian and Ellice considered only private centers. Publicly supported centers were not included as possible choices. They also plan to send their children to private, rather than public, schools "unless the Board of Education cleans up their act rather drastically. The educational system here is pathetic."

Brian feels a day care center is the best place for his children. He emphasized his belief that learning to be with other children in a center is a necessary preparation for kindergarten.

> I think it's better for the kids to be in day care. If the kid's alone with one parent, then they never learn how to relate to their peers. Then, when they get to kindergarten, they panic in the doorway. Because for 5 years they've been one-on-one with one adult. And now they've gone into a room with 30 kids. And they're expected to relate. Ridiculous!

Later in our interview Brian again made a point about socialization in explaining why he preferred center-based care for his children to having a home-based babysitter. He wants an "active social life" with a "mixture of peers" for his children and thinks that their staying at home would be "too dull" because there's "no activity."

Regarding housekeeping, Brian and Ellice find that "things go best when we divide duties." By agreement Brian is the family accountant, cook, and car mechanic. Ellice is responsible for the laundry and for cleaning the house. They split child care duties—on weekends Brian takes responsibility for the children on Saturday, and Ellice takes her turn on Sunday. When they need an evening babysitter they use church members they know—older German grandmothers whose children have moved away and who don't accept payment, or teenagers who charge $5 an hour. Brian's parents occasionally babysit, and it is taken for granted that they would accept no payment.

Before I left, Brian wanted me to see his older daughter's playroom, a small room adjoining the kitchen where dolls and stuffed animals were placed neatly in a row as though they were watching the large television set across the room. What Brian particularly wanted to show me was how his daughter played "day care." To demonstrate, Brian took two infant "burp pads" and put them on the floor. He then took down a couple of the dolls and placed them face down on the pads, while explaining that this is what his daughter does and that for a while her parents couldn't figure out what she meant. They finally realized that she was recreating nap time at the center, when the children rest on mats on the floor. Brian was pleased by this imaginary play and proudly reported that the little girl also runs videotapes for her dolls, just as the teachers in the center do for the children each afternoon.

GITA: FAR FROM HOME

Finding an Indian family who arranged for child care outside the family was difficult, but I finally reached Gita by a circuitous route. I had asked Brian for the names of Indian families with children, and he referred me to a liberal-minded "American" lawyer who worked with Indians on issues of tenants' rights. The lawyer, in turn, gave me the name of an Indian colleague. When I telephoned this man and asked him for names of Indian families I could interview about child care, he gave me the names of several men, all fathers of young children. He took it for granted that I would be talking to fathers as spokesmen for the families rather than to mothers. However, when Gita, rather than her husband, answered my telephone call, I persuaded her to be interviewed, even though she protested in a self-effacing way that her husband knew much more than she did about child care.

Gita lived in a rundown tenement building on a block known for its concentration of Indian families. In the dingy entryway, broken mailboxes all bore Indian names. I waited a long time for the buzzer to be answered, growing increasingly apprehensive about finally being able to reach an Indian family. After I had identified myself through the intercom, I climbed the stairs to Gita's apartment, which occupied the entire second floor and consisted of four rooms. On opening the door, Gita explained that she had expected me an hour later but asked me to come in. Behind her I could see a kitchen with a table for eating. Clotheslines strung with towels crisscrossed the ceiling, and a pungent smell of Indian spices came from pots on the stove.

Gita led the way through two small interior rooms that had no windows. The first was a bedroom with a double bed that took up almost all the space. The second was a cramped sitting room, where we talked. This room was furnished with a small upholstered couch and matching chair, much lower to the floor than I am used to, a very large television set, and space heater (the apartment is not centrally heated), and a table holding Indian periodicals. A single bare lightbulb dimly lit the room.

A curtained doorway led to the front bedroom facing the street. Explaining that she had been comforting her son who was suffering from a stuffy nose and that she now wanted to put him down to sleep, she retreated into the curtained bedroom, where I could hear her crooning a lullaby at his bedside. When she re-entered, I saw that Gita was a pleasant-faced young woman in her early twenties dressed in a form-fitting red dress. Her hair, parted in the middle, was smoothly looped behind her ears. Centered between her eyebrows was a round scarlet dot. She wore no jewelry and her feet were bare. She spoke in a low, soft voice, but her English was competent and she rarely paused to search for a word.

Gita began by explaining again that her son, who would turn three that month, had been sick with a cold. Almost predictably, the child soon began to cry from his bed, so Gita brought him into the sitting room, where she held him on her lap, head cradled against her shoulder, and stroked his hair. The boy appeared slight and listless. During the interview he seemed to take no interest in the talk and dozed, changing his position occasionally but never attempting to leave her lap.

At the time of our interview, Gita had been in East Urban for 4 years. She had come from a town near Bombay, where other East

Urban Indians also come from. A high school graduate, she was then working 3 days a week as a secretary; her husband, a college graduate who won first honors in India, had been employed as an accountant since coming to the United States. Both worked in the City. Gita pointedly told me that she didn't *have* to work but chose to in order to practice her English and to gain familiarity with American ways.

When Gita's son was born, her mother-in-law moved in, took care of the baby, and did the cooking. After 3 months Gita returned to her job full-time, 5 days a week. She preferred returning to work to staying at home with her son during his infancy. "It was not important," she explained, "because he was so tiny. And my mother-in-law was here, so I wasn't that excited about staying home. But once he started to talk, then I wanted to be home with him." Gita became increasingly more concerned about staying at home to care for her son as he grew older. When he turned two, she decided to cut back her work to 3 days a week to spend more time with him. "Now he goes crazy for me when I come back from my job, and he cries when I leave. He wants to be carried all the time," she reported with some satisfaction. "When he was tiny he would just feed and sleep, but now I can teach him something, like manners, and tell him stories."

When Gita's mother-in-law returned to India, Gita put her son in a private day care center, the Learning Center, for the days when she went to her job. "I was planning to put him in day care anyway," she said. "I have relatives, but I don't use them. I want day care so that he will learn this country's people, language, and have friends to play with." She also values the "nice activities of cutting, crafts, and singing songs" and contrasts these with her own ways of caring for her son. "They have good ideas. I don't have those ideas." She explained that during her days at home she sits on the couch and holds him on her lap as they watch television together or she tells him Indian stories. And she keeps him indoors because she considers the East Urban winters too cold to go out.

Gita and her husband view the day care center as analogous to private schools in India, which take children as young as two or three. They hope the center will provide their son with the skills in English he will need for school in America. Other Indian parents, Gita said, think that their children can begin first grade and then learn English, but "I see the children crying and I think it is because they can't understand the language." Her son, Gita said with conviction, will "definitely" go to college. She said that her husband, who is "very brilliant," believes in teaching their son and has already taught him the alphabet and to count to 25.

When I asked whether she had thought of applying for publicly funded day care, Gita answered that she briefly considered it, but she understood that she would have to fill out forms and wait to be admitted. (She was on the waiting list for the Learning Center for one month.) She was also concerned that her son be considerately treated for his chronic constipation since he couldn't make his needs known in English and she was more confident that a private center would provide this "nice care." When I asked about the expense of a private center she was taken aback and emphasized that they were not a family in financial need. She claimed that she hadn't given the cost any thought. Her husband, she assured me, is the one who deals with "all the money and things."

In the year since her mother-in-law returned to India, Gita and her husband had never used a babysitter. If they go out at night, they go where their son likes to go—to the temple or to a fast food restaurant—and they take him with them. "If I go, I proudly take my son" is the way Gita put it. If the couple attends a business function where wives are invited, they take the child along. They appear not to seek time to be by themselves. Gita quoted her husband: "My son must be with me at the time of my enjoyment.'"

Gita said that since she cut her work week to 3 days to spend more time with her son, she was bored. "There is not enough social activity." In India, she explained, "our culture is 100% different." She said that in India there was no divorce and most people live in "joint families." Although the wives do not work, grandparents who live in the household take care of the children. Families live in "separate houses with more space," and since the weather is warmer, people "can get together out of doors in small gardens, watching their children and talking together." Gita has evidently been less successful than her mother-in-law in making friends in East Urban. She said her mother-in-law took her grandson to the park every summer evening after supper, where she met friends and talked in the cooler hours of the day. Gita, on the other hand, complained, "I don't have enough neighbors" (although she had told me earlier there were 80 Indians living on her block).

When I later had a chance to ask the director of the Learning Center how Gita's son had fared, she said that he was the only Indian child in the center and that although he did not speak he appeared to understand. At first he cried "all the time," she said; then he cried only in the mornings and finally stopped altogether. But by that time his mother had decided to return with him to India, at least temporarily. The day care director was a little put out by this—after all the effort she had put into getting him to stop crying.

YOLANDA: SETTLING FOR LESS

I found Yolanda through a social worker who ran a support group for mothers who lived in East Urban's subsidized housing projects. The group had been formed under the auspices of the community mental health program of East Urban's hospital to give mothers a chance to talk together about child rearing or other family problems. Yolanda, who lives in the projects and who had worked with preschool children as an aide in East Urban's Head Start program, was hired to assist with the children's play group that was organized in connection with the mother's group. While the mothers met in one room, Yolanda, under the direction of a professional teacher, cared for the children in an adjoining room. Yolanda is Hispanic—her parents came to East Urban from Puerto Rico.

I interviewed Yolanda in her apartment. Like the other project buildings, it is light brick with an unadorned, utilitarian look of the least imaginative low-cost housing. The project's only saving grace is that the buildings are almost all low-rise. Yolanda's apartment is in one of the tallest, and she is at the top of the seventh floor. The building has no lobby, only a hallway in need of paint and covered with felt marker graffiti. The tiny elevator took a long time to come and an even longer time to move slowly up to Yolanda's floor.

Yolanda, a small, plump, friendly woman, greeted me warmly and asked if I had been frightened by the building's appearance. I somewhat dishonestly said no, and she said that many people were scared by the look of the place, but that actually it was not unsafe. The biggest problem, she said, was the noise, particularly at night when music blasts from oversized speakers, causing the bass notes to thump through the walls. She led me into the apartment, past a tiny kitchen where a pot of soup was simmering on the stove and into the living room, where the interview took place. She indicated that I was to sit on a plastic-covered upholstered sofa, which appeared to be on the "company" side of the room. She chose a shabbier couch opposite. Unwatched, a morning game show blared from the television set until I asked if it could be turned off because of my tape recorder.

Yolanda began by introducing me to her youngest child, Angel, who is two. Although she urged him to say hello, he shyly clung to her legs and hid his face. She apologized for his reluctance and said he was shy because she had stayed home with him, the youngest of her children. During the interview Yolanda kept him quiet by feeding him and then holding him until he finally fell asleep, sprawled half across her lap and half across a pillow she had placed on the couch next to her. I had the impression this apartment building was filled with busy, social activity. During the interview the telephone rang several times, and two women dropped in unannounced. The first came to make a telephone call, since her own phone had been disconnected, and the second came to look out of Yolanda's front window to see who had been pressing her buzzer from the ground floor.

Yolanda has four children—Alfred, 19; Luz, 12; Roberto, six; and Angel, two. She worked at various jobs before she had children but quit at the birth of her first child. "I wanted to go back to work," she explained, "but the only one that I trusted to babysit at the time was my mother, and she refused to do it. She felt like she was going to be a built-in babysitter when she didn't want to." Yolanda says her husband is "very loving with the kids" but that child care is her responsibility. She attributes his "macho" attitude to his Central American upbringing.

Yolanda returned to work when Alfred was five and in full-day school. She was living in Puerto Rico at the time, and since the school was right across the street Alfredo could walk home by himself and stay with a neighbor for about a half an hour before Yolanda returned from her work in a program similar to Head Start. After her second child, Luz, was born, Yolanda moved back to East Urban. She stayed at home until Luz was four and then took a job in the East Urban Head Start program so that she could take Luz with her to work. When Luz started full-day public school she was cared for by neighbors from 2:45, when she came home from school, until after 4:00, when Yolanda finished her work at Head Start.

Yolanda continued to work at Head Start through the birth of her third child, Roberto. She used a neighbor across the hall to care for Roberto when he was an infant, but there were problems.

> She [the neighbor] moved a couple of blocks away. Then I would have to pack him up in the morning and drop him off. She took care of him until he was about a year old. One day—it was 2 weeks before summer vacation, I remember—I had gone to pick up Roberto, and when I got there I found that his face was marked. I asked her what had happened, and she was in a very bad mood, and she tells me, "I fell down, and he hit himself on the cabinet." I just looked at her. The redness was all over his face. It was like somebody had just slapped him from side to side. The child was so depressed. I had noticed the change in him. I get the chills just talking about it and remembering. I went home and looked him over, and I cried. I never

took him back. I told my husband that day, "If we don't get
another babysitter for him I am going to stop working."

During the 2 weeks remaining until Yolanda's vacation from Head
Start, her husband's stepmother stayed with the family to babysit for
Roberto. She turned out to be "another problem." She would take the
child along when she visited her friends, which Yolanda did not object
to, but would forget to feed him. Although Yolanda provided canned
food for the baby he was often fed only crackers because the stepmother did not take the time or trouble to heat up the baby food.
     In the fall when Yolanda went back to work at Head Start, she
found another babysitter.

> She was a good person as far as feeding him. She had him
> really nice and clean when I picked him up. But she took care
> of four or five other children, and one day I noticed on Rober-
> to's leg there were scars, like a bite. That was on Friday. On
> Monday when I went back, I told her that there was a mark on
> Roberto's leg. I showed her. She said, "I'm not aware of any-
> thing that happened. But I do take care of a little boy that used
> to have the habit of biting, but I took that habit away from him
> by smacking him in the mouth. But if that's so, I'll have to
> watch him." A couple of days later Roberto came home with a
> bite on his back. A deep bite. When I took him over in the
> morning, I asked her. She said it was the little boy, and she had
> spanked him. She said, "I don't know why the little boy bites
> him, because he's a very well-behaved little boy. Your little boy
> doesn't bother him. He just sees him and he wants to bite. He'll
> go over and bite him." I was really upset. She kept taking care
> of the boy, and I tried looking for another babysitter. I didn't
> find anybody else. I had to leave him there. He went through a
> lot of things like that. One time he had his fingers smashed in
> the door because there were so many kids she took care of. The
> older ones that were her own, that she took care of in the after-
> noon, weren't aware of the little ones when they went in and
> out. That's the way it went all the time. After that I had to get
> another babysitter.

Yolanda again changed babysitters. The next babysitter did not
keep Roberto as clean as Yolanda wanted. The babysitter would
change Roberto's diapers, but she didn't wash his hands or face or
bathe him. Yolanda also felt she didn't feed Roberto properly. Yolanda

would give the babysitter food for Roberto, but the babysitter used the food for her own child instead. Yolanda once found the babysitter's child eating a can of spaghetti and meatballs that she had brought, while Roberto had been given only a small bit of spaghetti mixed with chopped boiled potato.

Around this time, when Roberto was almost four, he was diagnosed as having autistic symptoms. Although babysitters had noticed that Roberto would become very excited in new situations, they had not thought this particularly unusual. Yolanda had noticed that Roberto's speech was not improving, but she attributed that to "all the abuse he had been going through" in babysitting arrangements. Finally, when a woman visitor seeing Roberto for the first time asked Yolanda, "Is there something wrong with him?" it "hit" her that there might be a real problem.

Yolanda entered Roberto in the public school pre-kindergarten program, but the teacher "couldn't handle him" and cut his school day down to 2 hours. Since Yolanda was still employed at Head Start she found a babysitter to care for Roberto during the rest of her working day. This babysitter was pregnant and cared for Roberto and two other preschoolers. In addition, after school she cared for her own school-age son and Luz. The babysitter's son knocked Roberto down, slapped another child, and fought with Luz. "I found the woman had no control over her own children," Yolanda indignantly recalled.

The most Yolanda paid for babysitting during these years was $35 a week, which she still considers a fair price. She supplied the food and diapers. "They go up to $40 and $45 and down to $30 and $25," she explained. "You're lucky if you find one for $30 or $25. Those are rare. You hear about them. Let's say somebody tells me, 'I have a friend. Maybe you can get a good price.'" Yolanda's babysitters took care of between one and six children, including their own. Some lived in the projects and some lived nearby. Some were receiving public assistance and some were married to wage earners.

When Yolanda's fourth and youngest child, Angel, was born, she left her job to stay home with her baby, not wanting to have to go through again what she had gone through with Roberto in making babysitting arrangements. For a while she became a babysitter herself for three children from one family. Their mother dropped them off at 7:00 in the morning, and Luz would take the older two to school with her. Yolanda kept the baby along with Angel. The mother picked up her children as late as 7:30 or 8:00 in the evening after dinner. Yolanda began charging $20 each for the three children, with the mother providing food and diapers for the baby. But because the mother was not only receiving public assistance but also living with a man and working (under another name), Yolanda thought she could afford to pay more. When the mother repeatedly paid Yolanda a total of only $20 to $35 for the week, Yolanda finally told her, "Listen, I'm sorry, but I can't deal with it."

Yolanda now works part-time, 3 days a week, with the play group, where she can bring Angel with her. Roberto goes to a special school, where he is happy and learning, until 4:00 in the afternoon. Yolanda's husband, at least for now, has a steady job as a machine operator in a paper box factory. With three children still at home, the family manages but has no extras. Yolanda says that she never goes anywhere without taking at least one child along. She would love to "get away," to be able to take a vacation alone with her husband to Canada, but can't afford to. She also needs an operation for gallstones but keeps putting it off because she doesn't know who would look after her children.

With all the problems Yolanda encountered with babysitters, I wondered why she had not considered using a day care center. "I'm thinking about it for Angel," she said, "but I want to wait until he's about three." She explained that she is afraid of possible sexual abuse because of what she hears on television (although there has never been a proven case in an East Urban center). When Angel is three and talking, Yolanda figures he will be able to tell her about any abuse. She also worries about Angel's getting enough to eat at a center—whether he will be aggressive enough to claim his full share.

As for infant care, Yolanda is "very leery" of putting babies in day care centers "because I feel an infant needs a lot more warmth." It "might cross my mind," she said, if she personally knew the caregiver in the center to be an "affectionate" person. Her first preference would be to care for her infants herself. If that was impossible, her second choice (despite all her horrendous experiences) would be care by a babysitter. If her children were "well adjusted and learning" she would keep them with the babysitter until they entered school. But she is also aware that children with babysitters "pick up" undesirable habits. She gave as an example a "very sweet" neighbor whose children "do things only as long as it's easy. But I don't know if that's the sort of thing I would want my child to grow up with because I always taught my children that I don't care if it's hard, you have to work at it in order to learn how to do it."

Because she has worked at Head Start, that is the program Yolanda knows best. Although she thinks the Head Start curriculum is a good one, she disapproves of what she considers "babying" the children; for instance, not allowing the children to go to the bathroom without adult supervision. In Yolanda's opinion, the Head Start children need more discipline from the program, since discipline, she says, isn't provided in the homes. She says that Head Start has a better reputation than the day care centers, which are considered "a last resort by most families," but Head Start's short hours are a problem for working parents.

Yolanda had never considered that family day care might be licensed, but when I described how the system works in other communities she thought it would be a good idea. "If they are licensed and run under certain restrictions," she said, "that would make a difference. You'd have more confidence in them. There would be more you could do if anything happened. These people would be more careful. I wouldn't have to worry about coming home and finding Roberto all slapped around because the babysitter was in a bad mood that day."

Yolanda struggles with a low family income and the needs of four children. A second income would provide much-needed additional financial support for the family, but Yolanda's employment has been undermined by unsatisfactory child care arrangements. Unable to use her relatives and distrustful of publicly supported day care centers (the only ones she can afford), she has had to rely on a series of neighbors as babysitters, including some who have physically abused her children. Her son's handicap has made child care an even greater problem. So far, Yolanda's employment has been limited to poorly paid, part-time work. She makes the best of her limited options by staying at home with her youngest child, except for a part-time, low-paying job where she can take him along.

PATRICIA: STILL WAITING

Patricia is a member of the mothers' group that meets in the projects and where Yolanda helps with the play group. Martha, the social worker who organized the group, had told me how the play group evolved. Her first idea had been for the mothers to exchange baby-sitting services—that is, one would attend the meeting while the other would stay at home with both their children. The next time the group met, the roles would be reversed. The mothers turned down the plan because they did not want their children left with other members of the group. (This apprehension was based on the grim realities of project life. One of the women who later joined the group had a child who died as a result of abuse inflicted by her husband, who was subsequently convicted of manslaughter.) The solution to the child care problem had been to start a play group for the children, which—since the mothers were present in the next room—would not require a day care license.

Martha, the social worker, had told the mothers that I would be visiting and would ask them questions about child care. I arrived early and helped the professional teacher hired to lead the play group to set up the children's room. She had placed a variety of equipment and materials, such as an easel with paint, housekeeping toys, and blocks, in inviting arrangements. She asked me to run to the nearby Spanish bodega to buy apple juice as a snack for the children. One of her objectives is to teach nutrition, but she already found herself at cross-purposes with the mothers on the subject. They wanted to eat pastry with their coffee, but the teacher considers pastry to be junk food and told the mothers they shouldn't eat it in front of their children. (This reminded me of the nutrition lessons and their apathetic reception that I had read about in my historical search.)

Martha began the meeting, which seven mothers attended, but soon turned the proceedings over to me. This was an awkward situation, and the mothers responded reticently—except for Patricia. The liveliest member by far, she talked with animation and humor, much to the delight of the others, who enjoyed her impressive storytelling abilities. Patricia, who is black, had brought along her two children—a 2-year-old boy and a year-old daughter—plus her 4-year-old nephew. Dressed in a new bright yellow sweatsuit that concealed her pregnancy, she talked extensively about her ideas on child care.

Patricia grew up in the neighborhood, one of 11 children. She now lives in the projects with her husband, who works at various temporary jobs as a "jack of all trades." When Patricia was 7 months pregnant with her first child, she put her name on the waiting list for infant care at the publicly funded Elm Street day care center. She never made it to the top of the list, and so when her second child was born, she reapplied. A high school graduate with typing skills, Patricia planned to start training "in computers" to qualify as a secretary.

Only recently, almost 3 years later, she received a letter from the center in reply to her original application, saying she should telephone if she was still interested in enrolling her son because they might have an opening soon. "So I never called," she said disgustedly. "I ripped the letter up. I wasn't interested in it anymore. I'm pregnant. I have another child. So I might as well stay home with these three."

At one point, after her second child was born, she lived briefly near the Johnson School subsidized center. Because her sister worked there, she knew that it was "pretty good." The center would have taken both children, and she was about to enroll her son when she moved to the projects. Although she had moved only about half a mile away, Patricia decided she could not make the walk to Johnson School with two small children, especially in the wintertime. She also dismissed transportation by bus as too difficult and by cab as too expensive.

Patricia believes (and the other mothers in the group concurred) that the only sure way to get children into the nearby Elm Street center is by "going to the county"—that is, to be referred through a caseworker as having children in need of protective services. These children, as I had learned from Donna, Elm Street's director, by law get top priority. Patricia described how some mothers voluntarily seek this route as a strategy for gaining child care services. Patricia, however, considers this a perilous bargain.

> I'm not going through the county because they come to your house when they feel like coming. If they see one little scratch on your baby they'll swear you beat the kids. They take your kids from you. I'm not going for that. Because I know every family that went through that, the county came and took their kids from them because they said they were child-abusing the kids or not feeding them enough. And you can't even discipline your kids. If you yell at them, that's part of child abuse. How are you supposed to discipline them if you can't yell at them or hit their hands when they do wrong? You do that in front of somebody, right away you're beating up your kid. I'm not going through that mess. No one's taking my kids from me. I'll stay home. I'm not that desperate to get them into day care.

One reason that Patricia applied to the Elm Street center was that she knew the program first-hand. Both her brother and her cousin as well as friends worked there, and she had dropped by the center many times. Asked what parents thought of Elm Street, Patricia answered, "It's got a good reputation. You don't hear anything about molesting or beating or hitting the kids. They treat the kids good over there." Comparing different centers and what she had heard about them, she said that some had a reputation for being cleaner than others. Elm Street, she said, was clean.

When I asked Patricia if she had ever heard of children being mistreated in East Urban day care centers, she answered:

You hear that. People keep saying that. I hear that when the kids don't listen or they use their attitude, they slam them down in a chair. Or they make them stand in the corner or something. And with the newborns I hear they've got the babies crying and crying. And they won't pick them up because they say the baby is spoiled. But you've got to be there. It could be rumors.

Patricia's criticism of the Elm Street center was that they "don't teach children. I see them having the kids play with the toys all day. Then naptime comes. They go to bed. They don't teach them how to write. When they're in a 4-year-old class, they should know how to write a little—like A or 1 and 2." However, she admires the way the children in the center learn to play and get along with other children.

Like other members of the mothers' group, Patricia would not consider leaving her children with "just anyone." These mothers did not trust many of their neighbors as babysitters. They cited drug abuse and boyfriends as potential problems. When they do use babysitters it is often on an impromptu and informal basis. They will send a child to another apartment in their building to be watched by a relative or a close friend. These arrangements are for a few hours only, unpaid, and often reciprocal. Patricia described what she looks for in babysitters.

How clean they are. Are they responsible? I don't like anybody hitting on them. That's one thing I don't like. I want to make sure they feed them. When I bring the food to eat, I expect them [the children] to eat. I don't care if they eat all of it, just some of it. Make sure they keep my kids clean. Things like that.

Several of the mothers said they wished the play group met every day and could be turned into a center. There had once been a day care center located in the community building in the projects. Patricia's mother had worked there, and Patricia, as well as her brothers and sisters, had gone to the center for lunch and for after-school care. She remembers her center experiences as "fun." Patricia would also like to see the play group grow into a permanent center. She admires the play group teacher for her patience "because these kids are little brats. All of them. They all want their own way. But the teacher sits them down and calms them down." Patricia brings her nephew with her to the play group (in addition to her own two children), because even though his mother is at home Patricia feels the boy is neglected.

After the birth of her second child, and still on a waiting list for center care, Patricia herself turned to babysitting. She babysat for her relatives, caring for as many as four children in addition to her own two. "I felt because it was my family I should do it. I felt sorry for them. They didn't feel sorry for me to do it for me, but I did it for them. They only had part-time jobs, so it wasn't full-day. I was home doing nothing because my daughter was just a newborn. That's why I did it." She charged $30 a week and appreciated having "some money on the side" for her own children.

> I got the money for my kids. Pampers and baby food and all of that. I wanted money in my pocket for when the ice cream truck came around. I hate to have them outside and see the other kids eating something in front of them as they stare. I did that for them.

After I had turned my tape recorder off and was talking to Martha about when we would next meet, I noticed that the mothers' group had begun to talk together on their own. It was not a discussion about child care but about men who were currently in prison. I was vividly reminded that child care is only one of many serious problems these women face as mothers.

TWO WAGE EARNERS OR ONE?

None of the families described here was headed by a single parent. Each had weighed the alternatives of increasing the household income by having both parents in the labor market, or of having one parent stay at home to care for the children. Of the four families, Brian's was the most prosperous. He and Ellice were both educated through graduate school and have established themselves in careers. Although their financial situation is undoubtedly helped by their church-provided housing, both are in jobs—minister and social worker—that are notoriously underpaid for professionals. Whether the couple could maintain their standard of living with only one parent in the labor force is questionable. Perhaps their parents would be able to help them financially if Ellice should elect to stay at home with the children. But in any case, Brian says that they prefer working full-time to staying at home. "We'd both crack up if we weren't working," is the way he puts it. They are also the only couple of these four families who make a conscious effort to equalize the household and child care work between them. Presumably they would consider the decision to pursue a career as a choice open equally to them both.

Gita's family lives in wretched housing, although her husband is college-educated and works as an accountant. Gita does not see herself as poor. It may be that as an immigrant she has different ideas about standards of living than native-born East Urbanites. Gita says that her salary is not a necessity—that she has the choice of going to work or staying home with her preschool son. She also had the option, until her son was two, of working full-time because she could leave him with her mother-in-law (in exchange for room and board). She decided to work part-time in order to spend more time at home with her child, yet she found herself missing her homeland and was bored. (These conflicts probably contributed to her decision to go back to India, at least temporarily, where she will probably give up her part-time employment but have a more satisfying social life being at home.)

Yolanda and her husband, with limited schooling and job opportunities, depend on two incomes. Yolanda also assumes full responsibility for child care within the family. She has tried to combine the need for a second income with her responsibilities for child care by taking low-paying jobs in Head Start and in the play group, where she can work and care for her child at the same time. Patricia's plans for entering the job market through computer training have been postponed because of the demands of her two children, and as she is now expecting a third child job plans will be further postponed. Her family lives in subsidized housing, and Patricia sometimes supplements her husband's sporadic earnings with in-home babysitting for relatives.

Except for Brian's family, the others, even with small earnings, have chosen to forgo income from second full-time jobs in order for the mothers to spend more time taking care of their preschool children at home. In these decisions some are following family traditions; others are not. Brian disregards his parents' disapproval of Ellice's working. Gita leads a completely different kind of life in East Urban than she and her parents led in India. Yolanda and Patricia, who both grew up in poor families living in East Urban, are familiar with the tug between mothers' employment and child care responsibilities. Their mothers, like they themselves, needed the income a second paycheck could provide yet did not take full-time jobs outside the home. Patricia's mother decided, like Yolanda, to accept a low-paying job in a child care program as a solution to the double burden of employment and family obligations. Yolanda's mother stayed at home to care for her young children, and this may have influenced her refusal to act as a babysitter for Yolanda's first child.

.WHAT TYPE OF CHILD CARE?

Nonregulated Care

Using relatives for child care is a real possibility for everyone but Brian, whose nuclear "American" family is isolated from his and Ellice's relatives. Brian, however, does have an available social network from which to draw babysitters—the church. In the absence of family, he turns to church members to enable him to find teenage and older babysitters. As far as his relatives are concerned, Brian admits that even if they were available for child care he would not seek them as babysitters because of family tensions—"they would drive me crazy." For Brian and Ellice arranging for child care outside the family is preferable to care by relatives.

Gita, Yolanda, and Patricia have both relatives and neighbors from similar family backgrounds living close by. For Gita the educational benefits of center-based care, even by strangers speaking only English, outweighed the advantages of using her mother-in-law or the many Indian relatives and friends nearby. Yolanda prefers care by relatives and neighbors to day care centers. Patricia, East Urban-born and one of 11 children, has an extended family living nearby and cares for her relatives' children although they have not been willing to do the same for her.

Licensed Day Care Centers

Although three of these four parents considered center-based care for their children, they did so for different reasons. Brian wants private center-based care for his daughters rather than care in a home because he values the group experience. He considers life at home "too dull" for his children and wants them be socialized to group life at an early age as preparation for their entry into elementary school.

Gita sees center-based care as a way of Americanizing her son, enabling him to learn English and the ways of a new country. Accustomed to private schooling in India that starts when children are two, she views the private day care center as an analogous educational setting, the first step toward the college degree she envisions for her son. She values the teaching "activities" as an alternative to the television viewing and storytelling that she provides at home.

Yolanda, like many of East Urban's Born and Raised parents, mistrusts day care centers. She fears possible sexual abuse of very young children in center-based care, and she enrolled her child in Head Start only when she worked there herself. She has moved her children from one babysitter to another, finally deciding to stay at home, except for bringing Angel with her to her job at the informal but professionally run play group.

Patricia has a long-time familiarity with centers. As a child she was cared for at a day care center where her mother worked. She trusts center-based care from first-hand experience. The center where she tried to enroll her first child is one where her brother and cousin worked and where she frequently visits. She values the center's teaching of social skills although she is critical of its academic content. Even though she readily accepts the idea of center-based care as a possible child care arrangement, she has not been able to gain entry. Because admission for her son to the Elm Street center was so delayed, Patricia has given up hope of gaining a place.

Caring for Infants

These parents differed in their opinions about infant care. Brian approves of center-based infant care and prefers to have Ellice return to her full-time job as soon as possible rather than stay at home caring for babies. He had no problem securing a space in a private center's infant program. Gita, who had a live-in mother-in-law available, preferred to use a grandmother's babysitting services for infant care and to care for her child herself when he was older—a reversal of the more usual American pattern. Yolanda would trust no one to care for her firstborn as an infant except herself or her mother. Patricia, like Brian, was willing to consider a center-based infant program, perhaps because she had no relatives willing to babysit. Although she applied for infant care when she became pregnant, no spaces became available.

Cost and Location

Brian and Gita pay full fees at private centers, and neither complained of the high cost of care. Yolanda would be eligible for a subsidized fee at a day care center but chooses not to apply. Instead she pays neighbors more, about $35 a week for the care of one child. Patricia would also be eligible for subsidized child care if she entered a training program, but she has no access to the center of her choice.

All of these parents made arrangements for their children that were no more than a few blocks away from their homes. Day care centers are conveniently located to meet these preferences; that is, subsidized centers are near low-cost housing, and private centers are in more expensive neighborhoods. But the small size of East Urban and its irregular patterns of gentrification enabled Gita, who lives in a rundown tenement, to find a private center only a few blocks away.

JUDGING QUALITY

Parents judge quality according to their goals for their children, and these parents differed in their standards and in their satisfaction. Brian is so admiring of the social skills his child learns at the day care center that he takes pride in her imaginative recreation of them during play. Gita's concerns are that her child's health problem be treated sympathetically and that he learn English. When I talked to her, she was satisfied with the private center-based care on both counts. Yolanda was so distressed at the poor quality of the neighborhood care one of her sons received that she decided against using any babysitters for the care of her youngest child. Patricia had confidence in the quality of her choice of a day care center, but refused to leave her children with neighbors for fear of physical abuse or neglect.

A striking aspect of these interviews is how little parents appear to demand from child care arrangements. Of necessity they must find arrangements that are affordable and within reach by whatever transportation is available to them. Beyond that, as they describe what they look for in quality, their standards are simple and straightforward. In neighborhoods of decay and neglect, parents look for cleanliness. In households where the cost of food is a major item, mothers want to be sure their children are adequately fed. In communities where families under stress bear the injuries of domestic violence, parents seek child care that is safe. In families of immigrants of color, parents seek child care where adults will treat their children with kindness and consideration.

Middle-class parents like Brian who are able to afford private day care centers take it for granted that children will be kept clean, that they will be adequately and nutritiously fed, that physical punishment will be forbidden, and that their children will be treated respectfully. Given a choice of two private centers, both with spaces available, Brian took the trouble to look at only one, although he had heard the other was "magnificent." For Brian, the fact that people he knew recommended the private centers was sufficient endorsement. He assumed that if middle-class parents like himself used these private day care centers, that was a guarantee of their quality. Gita likewise assumed that a private day care center would have standards similar to the private schools she knew in India. When parents can afford to buy the best, this reasoning goes, the best will be supplied to them. As a result, these parents did not appear to look critically at their children's programs or to suggest improvements. They gratefully accepted what was offered.

Yolanda and Patricia operated under no such assurances. Experience had taught Yolanda that children left with babysitters could be subjected to uncleanliness, underfeeding, neglect, and physical abuse. She feared centers because of the threat of sexual abuse. Patricia trusted only those day care centers with strong community ties—where she had relatives and had personally inspected the program through repeated visits. Parents forced to choose the least expensive care are in no position to upgrade quality. If arrangements prove harmful they look elsewhere, leaving vacancies that are soon filled by other needy parents. If worse comes to worst, they make the necessary financial sacrifices to stay at home and care for their children themselves.

FOUR FAMILIES

These families are playing out four variations on the themes of work, family, and child care in the city of East Urban. For every family there is a different story, a different set of circumstances, different choices to be made. Behind the national statistics of increased participation of mothers in the labor force and the scarcity of suitable child care lie uncountable numbers of individual decisions and sacrifices required in an effort to accommodate what have proved so far to be irreconcilable realities of American family life.

Examining a single group in East Urban, the Born and Raised, enlarges our understanding of how people sharing a common heritage within a particular neighborhood also share assumptions about child care. Other groups—middle-class professionals, Indians, Hispanics, blacks—also hold child rearing beliefs in common. But American society is not only particularized into groups and classes; it is also a hodgepodge resulting from economic and social change. Families move around, intermarry, get a better or worse education, move up or down the job ladder, absorb information from one medium or another. Although ties to the past are strong, what worked before may no longer serve. Each family must to some extent carve out its own destiny, weighing the consequences of one course against another. In the case of child care, these choices in East Urban are too seldom without a cost.

Chapter 8

What Can Be Learned from East Urban?

This study is based on a limited number of interviews, but the same social and economic forces that shape East Urban parents' and caregivers' lives are at work in the lives of many others living in similar cities. Studying child care in East Urban raises issues that should be considered in forming child care policy. Foremost among these is regulation. Of the various forms of child care described in this study, which should be subject to regulation? In making policy decisions, should care by parents and relatives be categorized with care by outsiders? Another major issue is deciding how regulation should be administered. East Urban, located in a state that has no mandated family day care regulation, can serve as a case study of why the question of regulation has produced so much ambivalence at the state level (Adams, 1990).

The task facing child care policy makers is to work toward a system that will address the needs of all working parents and their children. Yet the national debate on child care has so far been largely focused on either middle-class, two-career families or impoverished families, particularly single mothers leaving welfare to go to work. The low-income, working-class families in East Urban represent still another large population who are in great need of child care but have been largely neglected by public policy. Women in these families also provide much of the child care in cities like East Urban, either for their family and relatives, for neighbors, or for upper-middle-class families.

In formulating child care public policy we must work to preserve and encourage what is good and functional about child care as it now exists in local neighborhoods and communities; at the same time we must eliminate the abuses and inequities inherent in the present situation.

CONCLUSIONS FROM THE STUDY

Parent Preferences

In the target study group, the Born and Raised, parents' preferences for child care within the family are strong and deeply rooted in cultural patterns. In these families, as well as other low-income East Urban families, parents are often willing to make economic sacrifices so that mothers can stay at home with young children. When arrangements are made outside the immediate family, the preference is for relatives, particularly the maternal grandmother, or for neighbors who are known personally or by local reputation.

Demand for Services

Increasingly, mothers of young children are by necessity seeking employment to support their families and to improve their household's standard of living. Beset by problems of increased costs of living (including soaring rents), low wages, sporadic employment, and separation or divorce, mothers as well as fathers are entering the work force. As a result, these working parents will need more child care.

Child Care Supply

At the same time, long-term and irreversible forces are shrinking the supply of child care in homes. Among these are:

> low compensation for child care services,
> opportunities for other employment,
> generational change and evolving roles within the family,
> changing residential patterns, and
> smaller families.

This inadequate supply of child care must be supplemented by an expansion of regulated family day care, especially for infants and toddlers, as well as of licensed day care centers, particularly for preschool-age children.

Babysitters

Born and Raised babysitters often provide affectionate, safe, reliable, and affordable child care. In this respect they perform a valuable public service and should be encouraged. On the other hand, they have little knowledge of the professional principles of child development, they are underpaid for their services, and they do not report their income from child care. Existing caregivers in this study have, at present, little motivation to become registered (which at this point is voluntary) and cannot be counted on to expand the supply of regulated care.

Quality Issues

As low-income parents by necessity seek child care from outsiders, or "strangers," they will have to rely on professional standards of quality rather than on personal and community-based, first-hand experience. They will also have to pay higher fees. Regulated family day care, subject to government standards and subsidized by public funding, would help to solve these problems.

Center-Based Care

East Urban's low-income parents increasingly seek early educational experiences for their older preschool children—not with relatives or babysitters but in licensed day care centers and in Head Start. These parents need high quality early childhood education programs in licensed settings at fees they can afford.

EAST URBAN AND NATIONAL TRENDS

When the preferences and trends of East Urban's parents are compared with Census Bureau statistics, the stories from East Urban are borne out on a national level, although the regulatory status of family day care varies from state to state. The latest Current Population Report shows changes over a 10-year period from 1977 to 1987 that parallel those in East Urban (U.S. Bureau of the Census, 1990). As maternal employment increased, care by relatives declined. In 1977, 35% of mothers of preschoolers were employed. By 1987 that figure had grown to 55%. During the same 10-year period the care of children under five by relatives (other than the father) declined from 31% to 22%, while the use of day care centers and nursery schools increased from 13% to 24%.

The Census figures for "organized child care facilities" include both "day/group care centers," which tend to have full-day care, and "nursery schools/preschools," which tend to have half-day programs. For children under five, employed mothers used day care twice as much (16%) as they used nursery school (8%), reflecting the need for full-day care. The latest report (U.S. Bureau of the Census, 1990) also notes that:

> The hourly demands for child care services placed upon families with mothers employed full time cannot normally be met by other household members or relatives who have full-time jobs and career commitments. As a result, the location of child care activities for full-time working mothers tends to be outside of the child's home and with non-relatives, rather than in the child's home with family members or relatives. (p. 4)

But while these changes are highly significant, the bulk of American child care arrangements, like those in East Urban, continues to be with family members and in family day care homes. This is particularly true for infants and toddlers. Only 14% of infants and 18% of 1- and 2-year-olds are cared for in centers or nursery schools. An even smaller proportion of school-age children (10%) are cared for in organized programs during nonschool hours. The increase in use of centers and nursery schools for preschool children, moreover, occurred between 1977 and 1984 (13 to 23%) and has since leveled off. For whatever reasons, the majority of parents are not moving their children out of home-based care, whether by parents, relatives, or other caregivers.

HOW MUCH REGULATION?

The stories of East Urban parents and child care providers are each a small part of the whole. Together, they form a mosaic in which we can begin to discern an overall view of the city's child care. What emerges is not horizontally stratified, with a small supply of licensed, high quality care at the top and a preponderance nonregulated, low quality care at the bottom. The picture is more complex and of interlocking parts, with children variously cared for by parents, relatives, neighbors, babysitters, centers, and preschools in overlapping and ever-changing patterns that are responsive to children's ages, family circumstances, individual preferences, and what is available and affordable. Not all nonregulated care is of poor quality. Care by parents and relatives, with the strong attachments it involves, is of course in a special category, and some babysitters are doing an excellent job. Nor can licensing serve as a guarantee of high quality; some of East Urban's day care centers are not as good as they should be. Broad sweeping statements about any one form of care being better than another can be countered with the experiences of individual families that prove otherwise.

Given the complicated web of child care arrangements in a city such as East Urban, it is not surprising that policy makers find it difficult to decide how much regulation is desirable for family day care. Questions of regulation are often framed from two different and polarized points of view. One side advocates increased regulation as a means of safeguarding children and improving quality; the other side argues that such measures work against family-oriented, informal care. The Children's Defense Fund (1990), for example, takes a strong position in favor of regulation as a "safety net to protect children" and as a basis for upgrading quality. It finds the high percentage of nonregulated family day care homes an "alarming" fact. The Family Research Council (1990) takes the opposite view, claiming that child care legislation with increased regulation "will establish new day care bureaucracies that will restrict parental choice" and "intensify government bias against family-oriented, informal forms of child care." Various predictions are made that one policy or the other will either expand or diminish supply, lower or raise fees, increase or decrease parent choice. The National Association for the Education of Young Children (1987), Reisman (1989), and Modigliani (1990), for example, state the advantages to be gained from increased regulation; while Haskins (1987), the Institute for American Values (1989), and the Republican Staff of the Select Committee on Children, Youth, and Families, U. S. House of Representatives (1990), describe the disadvantages. The stories from East Urban illustrate how hard these questions are to answer and how neither extreme view is entirely justified.

REGULATION AND SUPPLY

Terminology

One of the difficulties in considering regulation is an understandable confusion about terminology. Just as not all nonregulated care is of low quality, not all of it is illegal. In fact, in East Urban no family day care is illegal unless it is for so large a group that it becomes classified as a center and so must be licensed. Most of East Urban's existing nonregulated arrangements would be exempt from regulation even if the state were to adopt more stringent child care standards. Parents and relatives are not regulated by government (unless their subsidy is being monitored), and family day care providers caring for only one or two children are usually exempt from licensing. In all but 15 states, family day care homes serving three or fewer unrelated children are exempt from mandatory regulation under a system that includes inspections (Adams, 1990). This is a considerable exemption. A recent large-scale survey of parents and providers found that the average paid family day care provider cared for only two children, 1.5 of whom were preschool-age and .5 school-age (Kisker, Maynard, Gordon, & Strain, 1988). Regulation would not directly affect these arrangements.

When states institute regulations for family day care (caring for children in an individual's own home), they license or register caregivers who meet standards that cover the providers themselves (such as no record of crime or child abuse), children (such as age and group size), homes (health and safety considerations), and programs (such as discipline or activities). Most states have a separate category for group homes or have ratio requirements providing that larger groups of children must be cared for by at least two adults. In general, registration is a system designed to cover all family day care homes by self-certification and is randomly monitored. Licensing implies annual inspection visits, although very few states that license actually make such visits (Morgan, 1987). Whether these regulatory efforts increase or decrease the overall supply of home-based child care depends to a great degree on how they are administered (Morgan, 1980).

Although some proponents describe regulation as a sure way to improve services, it is not a guarantee of high quality (Young & Marx, 1990). Nor does regulation always result in increased professional training. Quality upgrading may be encouraged through financial incentives or by raising standards, but regulation alone cannot sufficiently address quality needs.

Family Day Care

If the state instituted mandatory standards for family day care, would East Urban's supply of home-based care increase or decrease? It seems likely, on the basis of what East Urban's babysitters say about their work, that two different kind of caregivers would then become available. One would be those traditional-minded women, such as Mary O'Malley, who see their role of "babysitter" as an informal extension of mothering. These women would continue to operate as babysitters, largely within the realm of exempt care, because they would care for only a few children from one family. The other category would be women such as Caryl, who would come to regard their work as a business and themselves as professionals. As licensed or registered family day care providers, they would be able to increase their earnings by taking care of larger numbers of children or charging more per child. Though they might be "strangers," they would be able to attract parents with the assurance of their having met state requirements. Communities sometimes fear that family day care regulation will inevitably work against family-like settings in favor of more center-like operations, but when regulations are sensitively administered this should not be the case. The overall effect of regulation should be to increase both supply and options that satisfy parents.

A major challenge to increasing the supply of regulated family day care in East Urban would be to overcome deeply-seated prejudices against any form of government "intrusion" on matters considered personal and private. Many East Urban women (and, probably, their husbands) would resist having to go through standard regulatory procedures that involved a great deal of bureaucratic intervention, such as submitting family members to checks for criminality; opening their homes to multiple inspections for safety, health, and licensing; filing tax returns; or receiving professional training. Yet other states— Minnesota, for example—have found ways to increase the supply of child care through regulation.

By using community-based people sensitive to local mores to help providers become licensed or registered, some cities have successfully encouraged both new caregivers and those already in operation to apply for family day care regulation. In Atlanta, for example, the Child Care Neighborhood Network runs a noncoercive program through local churches that has encouraged black, low-income former "babysitters" to become licensed; and in Santa Cruz, the California Child Care Initiative has successfully recruited new family day care providers from a Hispanic population (Lurie, 1990). Elsewhere, states have made efforts to reduce unnecessary duplication of inspection and to employ former providers as registrars. In these programs a key component has been a conscious effort to build trust by meeting caregivers on their own terms.

Such results do not come easily. Trust is not built overnight, nor does sensitivity come without effort. In Santa Cruz, for example, a Spanish-language director from the county Office of Education spends at least 2 hours going through the child care applications with potential providers and half a day "walking them through every step of a home health and safety check." The required fingerprinting is done by a woman who is part of the program rather than by an outsider (Lurie, 1990). Similar culturally sensitive efforts would be required in East Urban for regulation of family day care to succeed.

The supply of regulated family day care will increase only if caregivers are persuaded that becoming licensed or registered is in their own best interest. It is certainly more desirable and less costly to attract providers into a regulated system than to punish them for evading it. It seems likely that the greatest advantage to becoming licensed, from the providers' point of view, is increased income (Nelson, 1990). Caregivers can raise fees if parents are willing to pay more for licensed care, and they can find additional children to care for through referrals from the state or from child care resource and referral agencies (which cannot refer parents to care that is illegal). Caregivers are also drawn into regulatory systems as a way to become eligible for insurance coverage and reduce the risk of liability.

In the case of East Urban's babysitters, other attractions of licensing might also be strong. Becoming part of a network of family day care providers could help to overcome the loneliness of the job. If training leading to a license were sponsored by local institutions, such as churches or ethnically based organizations, women might feel more comfortable about making child care a more formalized business enterprise. If child care trainers could provide caregivers with services such as toy and book lending, or relieving caregivers while they took a break, far more babysitters might join the regulated system.

THE COST OF CARE IN A DIVIDED SYSTEM

Race, Ethnicity, and Class

Most of the interviews in this study were with whites, rather than with people who identified themselves as Hispanic or black, but a visitor studying East Urban soon learns about the various racial and ethnic factors that crosscut the city's social fabric, including divisions in how families care for their children. Ethnic and racial distinctions are highlighted when relatives and friends of the same background turn to each other for help. But these separations also exist in East Urban's licensed day care centers. La Casa, with roots in the Hispanic community, draws the greatest proportion of Spanish-speaking families; Elm Street, located near the public housing projects, draws the greatest number of blacks; and Johnson School draws more white families than the other two. The two private centers are almost entirely white.

But a closer analysis raises questions about the extent to which these apparent ethnic and racial divisions are actually based on an underlying structure of social and economic class (recognizing that these factors are, of course, linked). Although arrangements with relatives and neighbors understandably run along ethnic and racial lines, care by strangers crosses these divisions. White professional career families in East Urban use Indian, Hispanic, and black babysitters. Born and Raised babysitters care for Asian children. Caryl, a black babysitter, cares for both white and black children. Michelle, who is Born and Raised, has used Hispanic babysitters. In engaging caregivers who are strangers, parents seek those whose fees they can afford. Although these babysitters may be of various races or ethnicity, they are always of an equal or lower economic class.

In East Urban's three licensed, publicly funded day care centers, regardless of their different reputations for children of one ethnicity or race, the majority of children are from Hispanic, single-parent households. This is not a choice based on ethnicity but a reflection of the economic structure of East Urban. Most of its poor families are Hispanic, and, of those, single-parent families are most in need of day care.

In East Urban's two private centers almost all the children are white, not because blacks, Hispanics, and Indians are excluded, but because almost all the families who can afford to pay the fees are white. The few exceptions—Gita's son, for example—are the children of professionals. Born and Raised families, though white, on the whole are not able to afford care in East Urban's private centers. Those who enter the middle class with increased incomes are likely to move to the suburbs rather than pay high rents for gentrified versions of the tenements in which they were born. This leaves the private centers with a population of young middle-class professional families whose roots are elsewhere.

Public and Private

East Urban's system of public and private centers exacerbates this separation between rich and poor. Although it may seem more efficient for the Department of Community Services to administer a child care program where all subsidized children are together, this segregates East Urban's poorest children into the three public centers. The situation is made worse when subsidized places are in such short supply that only the neediest families are admitted to programs and only on the condition that they remain needy.

The Born and Raised families interviewed for this study found themselves caught in the middle between private centers whose fees they could not afford and public centers that admitted families whose low income qualified them for publicly subsidized child care. Yet even when Born and Raised families earned so little that they would be entitled to reduced fees in public centers, they often sought other solutions. This resistance appears to be a matter as much of economic class as of prejudice against families of color.

In East Urban, as elsewhere in America, day care has been rooted in a social welfare system for poor and dysfunctional families; in contrast, preschool educational programs have been mainly for children of the middle and upper middle classes (Cahan, 1989). Public day care's history in East Urban is not associated with families of color (the Community Day Nursery was for white children), but rather with families in need of welfare services.

It is because Born and Raised parents do not want their children in the same program with those in need of protective services, or those from families on welfare, that they are so resistant to public day care. As Gans (1962) wrote of the Italian-Americans he studied in the West End of Boston, "West Enders want for their children what they want for themselves—a secure existence as persons who are both accepted and somewhat envied members of their family circle and peer group. . . . The major hope is that in education, occupation, and general status, the child will not fall below that of his peers" (p. 60). The Born and Raised community, like other ethnic groups, prides itself on providing for its own through family and community solutions to avoid "public charity" (Yans-McLaughlin, 1977).

Middle-class families, secure in their high economic expectations for their children and able to provide rich school-preparation experiences in the home, are less vulnerable to these fears (Cochran-Smith, 1984). Moreover, the private centers that are used by middle-class parents identify themselves with a heritage of middle-class nursery schools geared to educational aims, rather than with the history of welfare-oriented day nurseries (Kagan, 1990).

If the supply of center-based care in East Urban were increased, and if more families were made eligible for subsidized care, programs would have a better mix of children. With enough centers to take care of all the demand from parents of all income brackets, the state would be able to purchase "slots" for income-eligible families in a variety of not-for-profit programs that would admit both subsidized and full-paying parents. Such a system would rely on community-based, not-for-profit programs, as distinct from centers like East Urban's current private centers, which are part of for-profit chains whose headquarters are elsewhere. The success of "mixed" centers, where children in subsidized slots are grouped with those of full-paying parents, would depend not only on whether a center decided that admitting subsidized families was desirable, but also on whether the state would be willing to pay a competitive full market rate for its slots.

At least some of East Urban's professional parents would welcome a mixture of families. One preschool teacher told me she had chosen La Casa, a public center, for her child after unsatisfactory experiences in the two private centers. She explained why.

> I happened to be in the park one day and I saw some children with two women who appeared to be teachers. They were Puerto Rican women, and I saw these kids—white, black, Spanish, Indian, Pakistani kids. And I said, now this is what I'm used to—a real mix. Those other day care centers were private and all-white, which is okay, but I didn't want my kid to be in an all-white day care center. It's not the way the real world is. I saw all these kids playing with each other and having a good time. I went up to one of the women and said, "Is this a day care center?" And she said yes and gave me the name of it, which is La Casa. . . . It was a priority for me to have a community-based day care center that reflected the community I lived in, and even the community in terms of the whole world. . . . I don't know why I hadn't thought to look into state- and city-subsidized day care.

Regulating family day care could also ease divisions along economic lines, so that poor children would not be cared for only by caregivers who were even poorer. If the state could purchase subsidized slots from licensed or registered family day care providers, more low-income parents—particularly those of infants and toddlers—would be able to choose caregivers on some basis other than who is cheapest. Regulated family day care providers could take care of children from a variety of families—some able to pay full fees and some subsidized by the state. A babysitter like Mary O'Malley, for example, might care for a mix of children—from parents like the Lorings as well as parents like the low-income Indians she turned away—if she were regularly paid at a government-subsidized market rate for the low-income children.

The shortage of high quality day care, whether in homes or in centers, along with the low income-eligibility for subsidized care, worsens the economic divisions in where families place their children. If more regulated, subsidized care were available, and if the eligibility guidelines were revised upward so that more working families would qualify for a fee based on a sliding scale, East Urban child care might be less divided by social and economic class.

PARENT CHOICE

Everyone concerned with child care policy, it seems, speaks of the desirability of parent choice, though the meaning may be quite different depending on who is speaking. Many opponents of regulation advocate parent choice in the expectation that parents will prefer care within the family, assuming that everyone has such an option. Many proponents of regulation assume that parents, given the choice, will prefer professional care, which will then replace family-like arrangements. The question, in either case, is whether advocates of parent choice would be willing to go along with what parents really want, or whether they are promoting parent choice in the hope that parents will choose only those child care arrangements that accord with their own preconceived ideas of what is "best."

In the case of Born and Raised parents, and also of East Urban's more recent immigrant groups, mothers often choose to care for very young children themselves if that is an economic possibility. These choices reflect family beliefs in the high quality of mother care, as well as a situation where women can find only low-level jobs that do not offer an attractive alternative to staying at home. Unlike well-educated, middle-class mothers, these women do not have the option of pursuing a stimulating career. If the family can maintain itself at a decent standard of living on one paycheck (or two with the father "moonlighting"), mothers may stay at home and assume the role of a "traditional" wife and mother. Of course, this is not always feasible and it is impossible for single mothers. When mothers are not available, parents turn to relatives and friends as the best substitute for mother care.

On the other hand, there are signs in East Urban of a growing acceptance of professional standards as a mark of quality in child care. Despite the availability of grandmother care, Suzanne decided to send her children to Head Start so that they would benefit from experiences in a group. Tina found that day care provided her son with school-readiness skills that he had not learned when he was in the care of his grandmother. Gita, by turning to center-based care for her son, deliberately sought American ways as a substitute for the family culture that had been reinforced by his grandmother's care.

In each of these cases, parents sought professional care rather than relative or babysitter care because they viewed it as educational and, on that basis, of high quality. To the extent that professional child care in East Urban is viewed as an educational institution for all families, rather than as a custodial service only for families in need of welfare services, it becomes more desirable to parents who are made anxious by the possibility of dropping to welfare status.

Funding Alternative Choices

To give parents a real choice in child care, it should be government funding policy to support a wide latitude of child care arrangements, including both regulated and nonregulated settings and both professional and nonprofessional care. Such a policy would make it possible for families to afford child care in whatever setting they chose. Refundable tax credits for low-income families with children would allow qualifying parents to make decisions. These funds could be used at the parents' discretion and so might be spent on any form of child care or used to enable a mother to stay at home. The nonrefundable dependent care tax credit is another means of allowing parents a range of choices. Under its provisions, middle-class families can claim child care expenses of any sort to offset a tax liability, as long as the caregiver's social security number is supplied.

Another approach to funding is based on the fact that high quality professional care is in such short supply that it is not a viable choice for many families. To make such care available as a choice to all families— not just those who can afford to pay high fees—government funds could be targeted toward high quality subsidized programs. Examples of such programs are Head Start and regulated centers and family day care providers who can demonstrate efforts to upgrade their quality.

What we do not yet know is how many families, given the choice, would prefer regulated or professional care to other arrangements. Licensed or registered care for infants and toddlers, for example, is in such short supply that we have few opportunities to learn how parents would react if it were made widely available (Child Care, Inc., 1989). On the basis of the East Urban interviews it seems likely that Born and Raised parents, at least, would prefer home settings, regulated or not, to day care centers for their infants and toddlers.

Another thorny question for policy makers is: To what extent should parents be protected from bad choices? Legislators concerned with children's welfare are reluctant to lend support to child care arrangements that might in any way put children in jeopardy. Under the Child Care and Development Block Grant, the major child care legislation passed by Congress in 1990, states must at least establish health and safety requirements for all providers who receive funds from the act. These regulations include prevention and control of infectious diseases (including immunizations), building safety requirements, and health and safety training for providers (Adams, 1990). Yet even these most basic requirements might strike many babysitters— such as Patricia, who lives in subsidized housing and resists surveillance of her affairs by welfare workers—as too intrusive.

The Role of Parents

To a large extent the success of expanding the regulated system also depends on parent demand. Middle-class parents, who might be expected to lead the push for regulation, have shown no signs of doing so in East Urban. Although parents like Brian take licensing for granted in the private centers they use for their children, parents like the Lorings have no qualms about using nonregulated care by babysitters like Mary. It seems likely that the Lorings and others like them would prefer to have a nonregulated babysitter who cares only for their children to one who runs a more professional operation like Caryl's with a larger group of children. When middle-class parents seek nannies or babysitters for their infants and toddlers, they want, as one parent described it, "a grandmother type" and would be unlikely to insist that a caregiver be licensed.

Parents in lower income brackets, who would benefit most from an expansion of subsidized, regulated care and of efforts to improve quality, do not, in East Urban at least, know enough about what their options might be to take a stand on the issue. As it is, with limited publicly subsidized care, they must settle for the least expensive care available. As a result, they sometimes find, like Michelle and Yolanda, that their children have been subjected to unsafe, unhealthy, or harsh conditions. Learning about the possibility of licensing family day care providers, Yolanda could see the advantages of regulation. Other parents in similar situations would probably opt for regulation if it were an affordable choice.

Since low-income parents have fewer means to provide educational experiences for children at home (Heath, 1983), these parents are increasingly persuaded by the reliability and educational advantages of professional care in centers. With increased parent awareness, they would probably come to see similar advantages to professionally trained family day care providers.

CULTURAL DIVERSITY

It is erroneous, of course, to assume that professional training produces caregivers who will act uniformly toward children. Lubeck (1985), in her study comparing a middle-class preschool with a white staff to a Head Start center with a black staff, found that teachers' behavior toward children varied markedly between centers. Teachers in the white middle-class preschool used an approach that encouraged individuality, while the black Head Start teachers encouraged obedience and group membership. In each program the teachers, though professionals, reinforced values they had learned in their own families.

How much continuity between care at home and professional care is desirable, and how much only perpetuates the present disparities in children's chances to succeed in the larger world, is a question that embodies one of the basic contradictions in child care (Joffe, 1977). But even Head Start, a program designed deliberately as early intervention, has been strengthened by parent participation (National Head Start Association, 1990). At best, these programs profit from teachers who learn home ways from parents, as well as from parents who learn school ways from teachers.[1]

In making the often fearful transition from child care within the family to care by strangers, parents search for arrangements they can trust and are often reassured by continuities between home and caregivers. At the same time, parents want the advantages of professional care if it means early childhood education, reliability, a healthy and safe environment, nutritious meals, kindness, affection, and fairness. If child care were to market itself as reflective of and responsive to community and family values, parents would feel more positive about leaving their children with strangers (Fitzpatrick & Travieso, 1980; Hill-Scott, 1986).

An account of how one East Urban parent learned to trust sympathetic, culturally sensitive professional care came from a Hispanic mother who moved her child from grandmother care to La Casa.

When I first thought about La Casa, my girl friend told me about it. We went in and stopped by, and I thought, "Oh, my

God—these people look like real Gestapo. They look so strict."
And then I went into the classrooms and I felt the warmth of
the teachers. Just the things that they do. When I went the first
morning they were feeding a little kid that didn't eat his breakfast. And I thought that was really nice. The cook was actually
feeding the child. I couldn't believe it. As far as I'm concerned,
they're number one. So much affection. The reason for that—it
may be stereotyping them—is because Spanish people are
known to be affectionate and warm. It's a family. We went for
a Mothers' Day lunch, and I was expecting sandwiches and a
cup of coffee maybe, and a piece of cake. And we had rice and
beans and salad and chicken! They took the time. You don't
find that around.

CHILD CARE POLICY

This study documents the fact that there is no one model of child care
that will answer the needs of all families. People will vary according to
what part of the country they live in and whether they live in a rural or
an urban area. They will also vary in what they want for their children
and why. These choices are deeply embedded in cultural settings of
family and community. In creating child care policy not only must we
act in the best interests of children, but we must also be responsive to
the wide variation in what parents need and want.

Nonregulated Care

Child care policy should support quality child care, no matter what
its auspices—whether by relatives, by well-known and trusted neighbors, by regulated family day care providers, or by licensed day care
centers. If we are to respect parent choices, we must also trust parent
judgments. We should realize the worth of care by relatives—that the
commitment and attachment to a member of the family and the sharing
of culture and values are prized by those parents to whom they are available. We should also recognize the validity of child care arrangements
that parents choose because they know and trust the providers. Although
these caregivers may lack professional expertise, they can serve to
socialize children to family and community values as well as provide
warm and caring surroundings. We should support these arrangements
with relatives and trusted neighbors by sensible exemptions to regulations and by tax credits for low-income families with children.

Regulated Family Day Care

We must encourage and support the growth of regulated (registered or licensed) family day care for those parents who have traditionally relied on relative care or trusted neighbors but who, because of the unavailability of such care or because of preference, turn to regulated and professional care. We must acknowledge that for these parents family day care—particularly for infants and toddlers—may be strongly preferred to center-based care. In expanding family day care, however, we must take into account that regulating home settings requires a familiarity with the positive values of such arrangements; a reduction of heavy-handed, bureaucratic, and intrusive procedures; and a sensitivity to cultural differences and family values. We must also adequately compensate family day care providers for their work—both as a principle of equity and as an incentive for them to enter the regulated system and become professionally trained. Working parents with low-to-moderate income must be helped to pay for regulated family day care by government-funded reimbursement on a sliding fee scale.

Licensed Child Care Centers

We must also continue the work of upgrading and expanding licensed child care centers. We should support a greater range of income-eligible families by expanding subsidized, center-based care and revising eligibility guidelines, so that families who need child care to improve their income will be charged on a sliding fee scale until they are able to assume the full cost. We should help to offset the income and the ethnic and racial stratification in these programs by encouraging a mix of subsidized and full-paying parents and by offering a sliding fee for low-to-moderate-income parents as they increase their earnings. We should define in the regulations the educational qualifications of child care workers for a career ladder progression, with increased salaries, so that day care will clearly qualify as an educational program rather than as a welfare service. We should make child care centers more responsive to local community values by encouraging professional teachers to learn from parents about local and family traditions, as well as having parents learn from teachers about professional practices.

The times urgently demand the formation of comprehensive and sound child care policies. But we must never lose sight of the families our policies are designed to serve. Only by building policies that also respect the social fabric of local communities can we expect to succeed.

Notes

Introduction

1. Fosberg (1981), reporting on the National Day Care Home Study, estimated that in 1977 5,214,500 children were cared for in 1,827,500 family day care homes, only 6% of which were in any way government regulated. Corsini, Wisensale, and Caruso (1988) estimate that more than 90% of family day care homes are operating outside any regulatory system. Professor Gwen Morgan of Wheelock College (in conversation) estimated that currently about half of family day care is regulated. She points out that this varies greatly from community to community, depending on such factors as regulations and the active presence of family day care networks.

2. See Glaser and Strauss (1967) for a description of how theory can be "grounded" in ethnographic data.

Chapter 1

1. For a description of relationships both within and external to working-class urban families, see Bott (1957).

2. Doumanis (1983) describes the evolution of mothering and child rearing in Greece from the collectivism of a rural past to the individualism characteristic of families living in modern urban settings.

3. For discussions of housework as a category of women's work, of which child care is only a part, see Lopata (1971), New and David (1985), Oakley (1974), and Rubin (1976).

4. Modigliani (1986) and Zinsser (1986) discuss child care as "devalued labor" and compare its earnings with those in other jobs.

5. Young and Willmott (1962) studied the effect on families who were moved from a London working-class neighborhood centered around life on the block to be rehoused in a suburban neighborhood where the scattering of kin, friends, and neighbors changed relationships, including those of child care.

6. See Nordberg (1985) for the results of a reader survey for *Working Mother Magazine* on this subject.

Chapter 2

1. For descriptions of Italian-American family life and attitudes toward outsiders see Gallo (1974), Gans (1962), and Peroni (1979). For an account of family life in an impoverished town in southern Italy see Cornelisen (1976).

2. Simon (1986) has described in her authobiography her experiences as a teenage girl from an immigrant family engaged as a babysitter for middle-class professionals.

> It was from her [the mother] that I learned a sort of child-rearing I had not known before: to persuade with respect in a calm, reasonable voice, to be truly, gently patient. Her concentration on the children's physical welfare and their behavior was so serious and constant that there was little tendency or even time for play. I supplied the games, the nursery rhymes, the stories, and the nonsense songs. (p. 41)

Chapter 3

1. For an account of how women's attitudes toward each other change when placed in the mistress–servant relationship, see Rollins (1985).

2. Nelson (1988) in a survey of family day care providers in Vermont found that

> family day care providers strongly believe that a woman's place is in the home (especially if she has young children) and that they locate their motivation for remaining at home in a personal commitment to being good wives and good mothers. They initially think their responsibilities to their families can be easily combined with their paid work. They soon learn otherwise. (p. 86)

3. Kohn (1969) discusses the differences between working-class and middle-class child rearing. Miller (1989), basing her conclusions on the language distinctions of Bernstein (1972), found differing perceptions of what children need according to the socioeconomic differences of day care personnel. She states:

> A child socialized to existence in a setting of poverty and inequality may have low expectations and low self-esteem but highly effective coping skills. The street-wise working-class infants in this study knew better than to touch the grating propped precariously in front of the electric heater or to roll off the diapering table when their teacher left the room. Naive, protected middle-class children would surely be unprepared for daily hazards the low-income children handled with ease. Children socialized to a life of privilege may be confident, verbal, and creative, but they may join the epidemic of adolescent suicides when the real world proves colder and harder than expected. (p. 93)

4. Heath (1983) compares the "speech communities" of low-income children with those of their middle-class teachers. Cochran-Smith (1984)

in a similar vein, analyzes "literacy events" in a middle-class nursery school setting and finds that teachers and parents share assumptions that lead to the children's early familiarity with books.

Chapter 8

1. Sometimes the problems of cultural adjustment are more easily seen in cultures other than our own. Dladla (1990), a South African trainer of child care workers, has described how she came to appreciate the richness, depth, and meaning of child care as practice in African communities, through the perceptions of those she was educating.

> I had started with the narrow idea of an expert, and ended with a more meaningful perception of an expert as a partner in learning. I rediscovered child care as I had known and experienced it as a child. During the process I learned the importance of theoretical knowledge; but above all, I learned how crucial it is to build on a community's knowledge and understanding. (p. 100)

References

Adams, Gina C. (1990). *Who knows how safe?* Washington, DC: Children's Defense Fund.

Aries, Philippe. (1962). *Centuries of childhood: A social history of family life.* New York: Vintage.

Bernstein, Basil. (1972). Family role systems, socialization and communication. In Dell Hymes & John J. Gumperz (Eds.), *Directions in sociolinguistics* (pp. 465–497). New York: Holt, Rinehart and Winston.

Bott, Elisabeth. (1957). *Family and social network.* London: Tavistock.

Cahan, Emily D. (1989). *Past caring: A history of U.S. preschool care and education for the poor, 1820–1965.* New York: National Center for Children in Poverty, School of Public Health, Columbia University.

Child Care, Inc. (1989). *No choice but home: Child care and welfare reform.* New York: Author.

Children's Defense Fund. (1990). States inadequately protect children in child care. *CDF Reports, 12*(1), 1–2.

Cochran-Smith, Marilyn. (1984). *The making of a reader.* Norwood, NJ: Ablex.

Cornelisen, Ann. (1976). *Women of the shadows: A study of the wives and mothers of Southern Italy.* New York: Vintage.

Corsini, David A., Wisensale, Steven K., & Caruso, Grace-Ann L. (1988). Family day care: System issues and regulatory models. *Young Children, 43*(6), 17–23.

Degler, Carl N. (1980). *At odds: Women and the family in America from the Revolution to the present.* New York: Oxford University Press.

Dladla, Yvonne. (1990). Rediscovering the meaning of child care. *Harvard Educational Review, 60*(1), 98–100.

Doumanis, Mariella. (1983). *Mothering in Greece, from collectivism to individualism.* New York: Academic Press.

Family Research Council (1990). Child care monster. *Washington Watch, 2*(1), 1.

Fitzpatrick, Joseph P., & Travieso, Lourdes. (1980). The Puerto Rican family: Its role in cultural transition. In Mario D. Fantani & Rene Cardenas (Eds.), *Parenting in a multicultural society* (pp. 103–119). New York: Longman.

Fosburg, Steven. (1981). *Family day care in the United States: Summary of findings. Final report of the National Day Care Home Study* (Vol. 1). Washington, DC: U.S. Department of Health and Human Services, Administration for Children, Youth and Families.

Gallo, Patrick J. (1974). *Ethnic alienation, the Italian-Americans.* Rutherford, NJ: Fairleigh Dickinson University Press.

Gans, Herbert J. (1962). *The urban villagers, group and class in the life of Italian-Americans.* Glencoe, IL: Free Press.

Glaser, Barney G., & Strauss, Anselm L. (1967). *The discovery of grounded theory: Strategies for qualitative research.* New York: Aldine.

Grubb, W. Norton, & Lazerson, Marvin. (1982). *Broken promises: How Americans fail their children.* New York: Basic Books.

Haskins, Ron. (1987). *Day care policy in the 100th Congress.* Remarks made at the biennial meeting of the Society for Research in Child Development, Baltimore.

Heath, Shirley Brice. (1983). *Ways with words.* New York: Cambridge University Press.

Hill-Scott, Karen. (1986). *Diversity . . . An approach to child care delivery.* Washington, DC: National Black Child Development Institute.

Institute for American Values. (1989). Everything money can buy: An economic analysis of child care. *Family Affairs, 2*(1), 1–7.

Joffe, Carole E. (1977). *Friendly intruders: Childcare professionals and family life.* Berkeley: University of California Press.

Kagan, Sharon L. (1990). *Policy perspectives, excellence in early childhood education: Defining characteristics and next-decade strategies.* Washington, DC: U.S. Department of Education.

Keyserling, Mary D. (1972). *Windows on day care: A report on the findings of members of the National Council of Jewish Women on day care needs and services in their communities.* New York: Day Care Council of New York.

Kisker, Ellan Eliason, Maynard, Rebecca, Gordon, Anne, & Strain, Margaret. (1988). *The child care challenge: What parents need and what is available in three metropolitan areas.* Princeton, NJ: Mathematica Policy Research, Inc.

Kohn, Marvin L. (1969). *Class and Conformity: A study in values.* Homewood, IL: Dorsey.

Laslett, Peter, & Wall, Richard (Eds.). (1972). *Household and family in past time.* New York: Cambridge University Press.

LeVine, Robert, & White, Merry. (1986). *Human conditions, the cultural basis of educational development.* New York, Routledge and Kegan Paul.

Lopata, Helene L. (1971). *Occupation: Housewife.* New York: Oxford University Press.

Lubeck, Sally. (1985). *Sandbox society: Early education in black and white America.* London: Falmer.

Lurie, Theodora. (1990). Increasing the quantity and quality of child care. *The Ford Foundation Letter, 21*(2), 1–9.

Mead, Margaret, & Wolfenstein, Martha. (Eds.). (1955). *Childhood in contemporary cultures.* Chicago: University of Chicago Press.

Miller, Darla Ferris. (1989). *First steps toward cultural difference, socialization in infant/toddler day care.* Washington, DC: Child Welfare League of America.

Modigliani, Kathy. (1986). But who will take care of the children? Childcare, women, and devalued labor. *Journal of Education, 168*(3), 46–69.

Modigliani, Kathy. (1990). *Assessing the quality of family child care: A comparison of five instruments.* New York: Bank Street College of Education.

Morgan, Gwen. (1980). Can quality family day care be achieved through regulation? In Sally Kilmer, *Advances in early education and day care* (vol. I), pp. 77–102. JAI Press.

Morgan, Gwen. (1987). *National state of child care regulation, 1986.* Washington, DC: National Association for the Education of Young Children.

National Association for the Education of Young Children. (1987). Position statement on licensing and other forms of regulation of early childhood programs in centers and family day care homes. *Young Children, 42*(5), 64–68.

National Head Start Association. (1990). *Head Start: The nation's pride, a nation's challenge.* Alexandra, VA: Author.

Nelson, Margaret K. (1988). Providing family day care: An analysis of home-based work. *Social Problems, 35*(1), 78–94.

Nelson, Margaret K. (1990). A study of turnover among family day care providers. *Children Today,* March–April, 8–12.

New, Caroline, & David, Miriam. (1985). *For the children's sake.* Harmondsworth, Middlesex, England: Penguin.

Nordberg, Olivia. (1985). The cost of child care. *Working Mother Magazine, 8*(2), 53–56.

Oakley, Annie. (1974). *The sociology of housework.* London: Martin Robertson.

Ochs, Elinor, & Schieffelin, Bambi B. (1982). *Language acquisition and socialization: Three developmental stories and their implications.* Sociolinguistic Working Paper 105, Southwest Educational Development Laboratory, Austin, Texas.

Peroni, Peter A. II. (1979). *The burg: An Italian-American community at bay in Trenton.* Washington, DC: University Press of America.

Pollock, Linda A. (1983). *Forgotten children: Parent–child relations from 1500 to 1900.* New York: Cambridge University Press.

Reisman, Barbara. (1989). *Child care welfare programs and tax credit proposals.* Statement before the U.S. House of Representatives Select Committee on Children, Youth, and Families, Washington, DC.

Republican Staff of the Select Committee on Children, Youth, and Families,

U. S. House of Representatives. (1990). *What America believes: The rest of the story*. Washington, DC: Author.

Rollins, Judith. (1985). *Between women: Domestics and their employers*. Philadelphia: Temple University Press.

Rubin, Lillian Breslow. (1976). *Worlds of pain: Life in the working-class family*. New York: Basic Books.

Ryan, Mary P. (1981). *Cradle of the middle class: The family in Oneida County, New York, 1790–1865*. New York: Cambridge University Press.

Simon, Kate. (1986). *A wider world, Portraits in an adolescence*. New York: Harper & Row.

U.S. Bureau of the Census. (1990). *Who's minding the kids? Child care arrangements: 1986–87*. Current Population Reports, Series P–70. No. 20. Washington, DC: U.S. Government Printing Office.

Werner, Oswald, & Schoepfle, G. Mark. (1987). *Systematic fieldwork* (Vol. I). Newbury Park, CA: Sage.

Whiting, Beatrice B., & Whiting, John W. M. (1975). *Children of six cultures: A psycho-cultural analysis*. Cambridge, MA: Harvard University Press.

Wishy, Bernard. (1968). *The child and the Republic*. Philadelphia: University of Pennsylvania Press.

Yans-McLaughlin, Virginia. (1977). *Family and community: Italian immigrants in Buffalo, 1880–1930*. Ithaca, NY: Cornell University Press.

Young, Kathryn T., & Marx, Elisabeth. (1990). *Do state regulations require child care centers to provide quality care by a well prepared staff?* Unpublished paper, Smith Richardson Foundation.

Young, Michael, & Willmott, Peter. (1962). *Family and kinship in East London*. Baltimore: Penguin.

Zinsser, Caroline. (1986). *Day care's unfair burden: How low wages subsidize a public service*. New York: Center for Public Advocacy Research.

Zinsser, Caroline. (1987). *Over a barrel: working mothers talk about child care*. New York: Center for Public Advocacy Research.

Index

Adams, Gina C., 158, 166
After-school care, 36, 42, 81, 83, 84, 108, 112, 122
Alicia (case study), 40–44
Ana (case study), 116–19, 120, 129
Angela (case study), 116–19
Aries, Philippe, 3

Babysitters
  alternative work for, 14–15, 16–17, 24, 52–53
  attitudes toward working women of, 19
  and child rearing practices, 26–27, 65–71, 75–76
  and children's activities, 21, 68–70
  and cleanliness, 62, 75
  daily activities/responsibilities of, 63–64, 68–70
  and day care centers, 17–18
  and domestic roles, 53, 63, 74, 158–59
  and economic class, 15–16, 27, 54–56, 57–58, 59, 73–74, 75–76
  and educating children, 27, 69–70, 75–76
  and family background, 65
  and family values, 53, 75–76
  fees of, 17, 19–20, 23, 29, 54–58, 73–74
  and good/bad children, 65–67, 74–75
  and health/safety issues, 62, 65–67, 74–75
  and housecleaning, 54–56, 62–63
  and husbands of sitters, 71–72
  and income tax, 49, 60–61, 74
  and in-home care, 54, 59, 61–64
  and legality, 50, 58–61

loneliness of, 64, 160
  as nurturing, 73–74
  and parents, 67–68, 70–71, 75–76
  qualifications of, 53
  and quality of care, 74–76, 77
  and reasons for sitting, 50–53, 73
  self-image of, 49, 53, 57, 58, 74, 81
  and sitting for relatives, 72–73
  training of, 65, 68
  turnover of, 45
  and working conditions, 61–65
  See also Born and Raised society;
      Family care; Grandmothers;
      O'Malley, Mary; Night care
Benefits, for sitters/staff, 58, 74, 121, 123
Bernstein, Basil, 3
Blacks
  and the Child Care Neighborhood Network, 159
  and day care centers, 108, 121–22, 125, 127
  and economic class, 148
  in housing projects, 144–47
  See also Patricia
Born and Raised society
  characteristics of, 5–6, 31–32
  discrimination by, 97–98, 101–2
  and fees, 121, 161
  and the government, 74, 102
  and neighbor care, 25–26, 28–29
  and outsiders, 23, 100
  and preferences in care, 23, 27–29, 49, 75–76, 93, 95, 100, 101, 105, 121, 126, 127, 154, 164, 165
  and public vs. private care, 161, 162

179

About the Author

Caroline Zinsser is a writer, a teacher, and a researcher in the field of early childhood education and an advocate for improving services for young children. As a contributing editor to *Working Mother Magazine*, she has written extensively on the subject of changes in American families. As a staff member of the Center for Public Advocacy in New York City, she was project director of the child care and early childhood education policy study and author of *Day Care's Unfair Burden: How Low Wages Subsidize a Public Service*, *Over a Barrel: Working Mothers Talk about Child Care*, and *One Hundred Working Women*.

Ms. Zinsser has been a public school classroom teacher in New York City and in New Haven, where she taught at the Martin Luther King school under the direction of James Comer. She has also taught courses at Yale University and the University of Pennsylvania in child development, early childhood education, the sociology of childhood, and urban studies. She has been director of St. Thomas's Day School in New Haven and the Bank Street School for Children in New York City.

Ms. Zinsser has held positions as a research associate at the Yale Child Study Center, as an associate in research at the Center for the Study of Education at the Institution for Social and Policy Studies at Yale, and as a Bush Fellow of the Council for Research in Child Development. She has served on the New York State Governor's Commission on Child Care, the advisory board of the Child Care Employee Project, and the steering committee of the Alliance for Better Child Care. At present, she is the on-staff education consultant for the Rockefeller Brothers Fund.

Ms. Zinsser holds a M.S. from the Bank Street College of Education and a Ph.D. from the University of Pennsylvania. She resides in New York City with her husband and is the mother of two children.